COLLECTED POEMS
1953–1994

COLLECTED POEMS

1953–1994

ERNEST SANDEEN

University of Notre Dame Press
Notre Dame, Indiana

Library of Congress Cataloging-in-Publication Data

Sandeen, Ernest Emanuel, 1908–
Collected poems, 1953–1977.
PS3537.A6233A17 1977   811'.5'2   77-22154
ISBN 0-268-00721-7

Sandeen, Ernest Emanuel, 1908–
A later day, another year.
I. Title.
PS3537.A6233L3   1989   88-33886
ISBN 0-268-01288-1

Sandeen, Ernest Emanuel, 1908–
Can these bones live? : new poems / by Ernest Sandeen.
p. cm.
ISBN 0-268-00808-6 (alk. paper)
1. Aged men—Poetry. I. Title
PS3537.A6233C36   1994
811'.52—dc20   94-25943

Sandeen, Ernest Emanuel, 1908–
[Poems]
Collected poems, 1953–1994 / Ernest Sandeen.
p.   cm.
ISBN 0-268-02268-2 (alk. paper)
I. Title.
PS3537.A6233 A6 2001
811'.52—dc21
2001001293

For Eileen

These marigolds, petunias, dahlias,
geraniums and daisies are from your planting.
Their reds and yellows wear your modest intensities.

I see your eyes love them below their small bright faces.
Their look tingles down your arms to the roots
you fingered into place in our springtime soil.

Do you know what love it is you were born for?
Your care, the slumbering earth, uses your eyes
to waken to its art of leaf and blossom.

I've loved you for forty years with fingers
that move from love in eyes down to the dark
where our two lives tangle in a root of flesh.

Yet I have merely secrets that I could tell
of you. Your privacies are names as slow as aeons,
they move in verbs too deep, too long for speech.

Contents

LATER POEMS (1976–1977)

A Later Day, Another Year:
Poems, 1977–1988

Entrances Haunted by Exits

Games Not to Be Toyed With

Natural Relations

FAMILY RELATIONS

FELLOW TRAVELERS

CAN THESE BONES LIVE?

Foreword

from *Can These Bones Live?*

The poems of Ernest Sandeen among other things record not only a writing life but a life *in writing*: a history of the hours when reflection turns to discovery, and observation finds its fulfillment in the rhythms of a sentence, the weaving of consonants through a line, in pursuit of a mystery. Few poets have been blessed with the gift to sustain that process of meditation, composing and questioning so consistently, and for so long, in works that are clear and clear-eyed, passionate and precise.

So it is with renewed wonder that readers can see the poet in his most recent poems regarding all that various, wide terrain, with gaze as clear as ever and still allured by the mystery, not flinching from it:

> *A Still Noise*
> There once occurred a silence,
> all dark and odorless, that commanded me
> to halt and listen. How could I refuse?
> And now after so many years ago
>
> how can I remember what I heard?
> I have waited too long: the dead
> have become too many and too explicit,
> and the living suspect nothing.

Much of the well-measured poetry of this poem hinges on the tough, perhaps startling word "explicit": the literal, exacting reality of those dead, like letters spelling a sentence the cloudy, unknowing living cannot read.

Explicitness that acknowledges mystery: that would be one way to define the virtues of Sandeen's writing. In "A Brief Story of Time, Outside and In" the explicit presents itself as a series of sounds, and the great mystery is embodied in what those sounds add up to for the perceiver:

> What he hears first is the unceasing, merciless din of traffic
> along the nearby highway punctuated
> with dissenting sirens. And then from across the river

he detects the church tower keeping the faith,
storing each hour away, melodious quarter by quarter.
What is left for him to do is to listen for silences

within himself deep enough to resonate into one
inexpressible meaning the fury of the pavement
with the meditative bell.

Meaning, even inexpressible meaning is the object of the poet's quest, and the poems have the confident wisdom to locate their grail in silence. In the poem "Soon after Nightfall," where the murmured, uncomprehended words of prayer are called "the wisdom of the Elders," that phrase is earned.

It is easy enough to invoke the names of silence and mystery; in this career they convince, because they are rooted in the daily noises of traffic and the wails of ordinary calamity. In this collection, nuggets and small, bright fragments of poetry find a place–held among those deep-going roots, the nourishing, soil-fed tangle that feeds the green crown.

Robert Pinsky

Introduction

Edward Vasta

Although Ernest Sandeen composed and published poetry for almost two-thirds of the last century, from 1933 to 1994, a history of American modernist poetry would place him in the twentieth century's second generation of poets, those of the '40s, '50s, and '60s. His contemporaries, to cite a representative few, included Robert Penn Warren, W. H. Auden (who became an American citizen in 1946), Gwendolyn Brooks, Denise Levertov, and Robert Bly. This mid-century group took its inspiration from the century's first generation of poets, such innovative and influential masters as Robert Frost, Carl Sandburg, Wallace Stevens, William Carlos Williams, Ezra Pound, and T. S. Eliot. From their elder's legacy, Sandeen's generation drew initiatives that turned the history of American poetry in new directions. They redefined poetry, developed new theories, published manifestos, and thereby opened up the art of poetry to the century's third generation: the Beat poets (Allen Ginsburg and Lawrence Ferlinghetti); the New York School of poets (Frank O'Hara and John Ashbury); Surrealist poets (W. S. Merwin and Diane Wakoski); and still other movements and poets of diverse interests, such as those represented by Anne Sexton, Adrienne Rich, Imamu Amiri Baraka (Leroy Jones), Thom Gunn (who, like Auden, came from England), and Derek Walcott (from the British West Indies). The broad-ranging affiliations and orientations of this third generation have produced a cornucopia of poetic subjects, forms, and styles.

To sketch Sandeen's generation further, but briefly, it begins with the development of New Criticism, a theory born as much from literary study as poetic practice. This theory emerged slowly and during the full flowering of such existing poetic commitments as Eliot's Symbolism, Pound's Imagism, Williams' Objectivism, and Frost's Pastoralism. Coming into full maturity and dominance in the 1940s, New Criticism declared that a poem, once composed, is a self-existent and self-contained verbal artifact whose qualities and meaning can be grasped and endlessly explored only by "close reading." Under its influence, poets of the middle generation, such as Theodore Roethke, Robert Lowell, and John Berryman, moved toward a controlled style enriched by metaphysical wit, but they still adhered to traditional forms. However, by the 1950s, in order to express sensitivity and sympathy as well as wit, but to do so through images and phrases that avoided sentimentality and sensationalism, the generation's university poets, who like Sandeen were also teachers and critics, developed more open poetic forms. Particularly noted in this regard are Richard Wilbur, Howard Nemerov, Louis Simpson, John Hollander, Elizabeth Bishop, and Josephine Miles. By the 1960s, finally, Charles Olson of Black Mountain College, whose faculty included Robert Creeley and Robert Duncan, produced a manifesto that called for Projective Verse, poetry that confronted the world directly and objectively, that conveyed these confrontations dynamically, and that let the rhythms of breathing govern lines and let the subject matter govern forms.

Ernest Sandeen spent virtually his entire life in the century's poetically generated culture. He was born on December 15, 1908, of a Swedish farm family in Galesburg, Illinois, home of Carl Sandburg, who was Sandeen's first literary influence (other principal influences were T. S. Eliot, Robert Frost, and W. H. Auden). He earned a B.A. at Knox College, a B. Litt. at Oxford, and a Ph.D. in English literature at the University of Iowa. Prior to undertaking doctoral studies, he taught at Knox College, where he married Eileen Bader. After doctoral studies he taught briefly at Iowa. From 1943 to 1946 he served in the U.S. Navy, then resumed his vocation as poet and teacher at the University of Notre Dame (he and his family converted to Catholicism in 1948). His long tenure in Notre Dame's English Department was interrupted by visiting appointments to the University of Aarhus in Denmark, the University of Minnesota, the English Institute in Hawaii, and Eckerd College in Florida. He died on July 12, 1997.

Sandeen's first published poem, "Parked Car," appeared in *The New Yorker* in 1938. After that, his works appeared widely in major reviews, journals, and magazines, including some three dozen in *Poetry* alone. They were also collected in six volumes: *Antennas of Silence* (1953), *Children and Older Strangers* (1962), *Like Any Road Anywhere* (1976), *Collected Poems: 1953–1977* (1977), *A Later Day, Another Year: Poems, 1977–1988* (1989), and *Can These Bones Live?* (1994).

The subject matter of Sandeen's poems came from daily life. As he wrote in the only statement he ever printed about his poetry:

> All I know is that they provide for me an intimately personal record: the poems tell me, as no diary or journal could, where I was at various times in my life and how it felt to be there. I hope there will be read-

ers who recognize the same places in their interior experience even though they may be far removed from me in chronological time.
(Preface, *Children and Older Strangers,* xiii)

Time is a preoccupation in Sandeen's poems. As "antennas of silence," they listen for "the sea of the seasons" and the "toss and hum of night and day." The poems bring life and death into presence through a personal consciousness that extends to other times, other places, other persons, and to material, psychological, and spiritual realms that extend to humanity's origins and destinies. The phrase "interior experience" in the above quotation is telling, for Sandeen's ultimate subject is the human spirit's condition as discernible in ordinary circumstances. In effect, Sandeen writes not merely autobiographically but, as it were, vatically, with the kind of insightful power given to poets over and above, as Sandeen saw it, their redeemed humanity. It is this understanding that makes his poems strikingly universal and authentic.

Such a consciousness can only be conveyed in figurative and tropological language and in imaginative rhetorical strategies. Sandeen's early poetry proliferates, sometimes densely, with similes, metaphors, metonymies, synecdoches, paradoxes, oxymorons, and such figures as conflate multiple realms of time, reality, and meaning. In his later poetry, his language grows plainer; rhetorical forms take on more of the burden of suggestiveness and ambiguity. Later poems make frequent use of personification and often push against parable, myth, and even allegory. Similarly, in his early poems versification is highly regular, although his skill in the rhythms of syntax and meaning disguise the disciplined control of meter, rhyme, and stanza form. His later verses are free, flexible, varied in form, and sometimes experimental in their prosody. His latest poems, especially those in *Can These Bones Live?,* written when illness and old age confronted death, are short, sometimes blunt, sometimes minimal.

Throughout his work, subject and style are integral to the guise in which life opens itself to the mind. The truth about his personal life, and life itself, is revealed to Sandeen in its ironies, paradoxes, binary oppositions, antitheses, and the mystery of contradictions—how they exist despite logic, for good and ill, once and for all. Such insights give his poems, often wry and humorous and commonly entitled with amusing understatements of what they present, an intellectual vigor that can be difficult, at times almost impenetrable, but characteristically convincing and always surprising. His intellectualism, operating so well through imaginative forms and expressive language, gives many of his poems extraordinary emotional power.

Although Sandeen described himself as a poet who, like Theodore Roethke, "learns by going where I have to go," and left it to others to find in his work a pattern of development and growth, his appreciable number of poems allow one to infer from them a consistent, developing poetics. Early poems in this group equate poetry with story, song, prayer, and thought—that is, with the various forms in which reality, or the truth of things, comes to consciousness through words. As noted, Sandeen's early poems are presented as "antennas of silence," which give voice to the underlying truths of life, and which address that voice to the poet as well as to humanity.

Later works use the word "poem" in two senses. The poem made of words seems to incarnate the creative foundation of life (suggesting, but never stating, that the poet's human words incarnate the Divine Word). "Poem" thus designates both the "antenna of silence" and the reality of life that the antenna receives and transmits. Poetic creativity cooperates with the force behind all creation, which in an interview Sandeen suggested may have an aesthetic as well as providential purpose. Conjoined with creativity's processes of birth and death, for example, the poet's poem constitutes a kind of unfleshing of the self even as the self lives.

This poetics reaches full development in *Like Any Road Anywhere* (1976). In these, the poem itself is metapoetically present as a personified character. "The poem has haunted most of my adult years," Sandeen wrote in a letter to a fellow poet, "The poem has always been there, troubling me, a kind of Platonic abstraction, I suppose, but always taking a concrete form." Now voiced and conscious, the poem is, in effect, reality witnessing itself being experienced. It observes and addresses the poet's persona, which gropes in the dark, struggling with its "story-thickened passions."

In many ways, the poems of Sandeen's last two volumes are his most powerful, particularly those of *A Later Day, Another Year*. As the title indicates, Time is the single theme throughout. Suffering from cancer and a relentlessly debilitating body, Sandeen meditated on old age and mortality, but his poetic meditations do not define conditions, nor resolve questions with answers, nor close down thought. Rather they open up the mind to more than the mind can know. They consider how the knowledge offered by the natural sciences, social sciences, humanities, the arts, and theology all lay out the comprehensible incomprehensibility of the earth, of life, of the universe, and of God. While Sandeen's earlier poetry is often straightforwardly religious, here God is simply a part of reality and Jesus a homely divinity. And all are treated humorously, sometimes with comic irony; a genetic disease, for example, is benignly addressed as a diligent, devout friend of birth who eventually becomes a skulking prowler that wants to take your breath away.

Mortality itself is the theme of Sandeen's last volume, *Can These Bones Live?* Here again, through scientific perception, humanistic sensitivity, moral reflection, religious faith, and divine inspiration, Sandeen projects an old man's consciousness onto the ordinary, inevitable, but incomprehensible facts of life. These short and simple poems are sometimes wry, but mainly serious; sometimes gloomy, but their details have large implications, their subtextual invitations are learned, and their subtle understanding and plain expression are brilliant.

The poetics implied in Sandeen's work, of which only the gist has been extracted here, seems thus both traditional and original. It evokes affinities with ancient inspiration, medieval spirituality, modern intellectualism, and post-modern skepticism. Yet, his poetics seems all his own, drawn not from any manifesto, which he never wrote, but from the potential of poetry itself. In this sense, as well, his work is universal and authentic.

COLLECTED POEMS,
1953–1977

Preface

from *Collected Poems, 1953–1977*

This volume of *Collected Poems* contains most of the poems in *Antennas of Silence* (1953), and *Children and Older Strangers* (1962), together with all of the poems in *Like Any Road Anywhere* (1976). The first printing of *Like Any Road Anywhere* is almost sold out, and it was thought that a second printing might well include the first two books, which have been out of print for some time. In this way the poems of all three books will be made available again in one package.

In their original magazine publication the poems of the three books included here extend from 1938 to 1976. Whether or not the poems over this long span of years show a pattern of development and growth is not for me to say. All I know is that they provide for me an intimately personal record: the poems tell me, as no diary or journal could, where I was at various times in my life and how it felt to be there. I hope there will be readers who recognize the same places in their interior experience even though they may be far removed from me in chronological time.

I feel toward those far-off poems in *Antennas of Silence* and *Children and Older Strangers* as most of us probably feel toward the earlier stages of our lives. We may be dismayed at the obvious ineptitudes and clichés we were then comfortable with, and amazed at the risks we took with such innocent abandon. But here and there we can only wonder at the strokes of sheer luck we enjoyed and at those incidental graces no longer within our reach.

To soften the ominous sound of finality in those two words "collected poems," I have added eighteen "later poems" written after the publication of *Like Any Road Anywhere* in May 1976. "What falls away is always," wrote Theodore Roethke, "and is near." Yet he knew that in the meantime the work is never finished, the initial imperative is still in force: "I learn by going where I have to go."

Ernest Sandeen
Notre Dame, Indiana, 1977

from:

ANTENNAS OF SILENCE
1953

The Rites

I carry him softly out of doors and for
the first time he understands the dark is more
of magic than house-contrivance in switch and lamp.
Because he's met night only by the roomful
I swing him up to sit manshoulder tall.
(What light of sky there is is curdle-damp.)

My ear guarding the little tower of
his stillness we follow a simple trail of love:
from lawnchairs the gate skims open to fin-delights
of birdbath and waternozzle. But seeing this dusk
has emptied their shine and chuckle he drops the husk
and peers far here, far there at speck of lights.

When mother calls from a sudden sill of gold
he wriggles off this thing of dark and cold
and big for chattering about it, inspired
by her nesting arms. Backstage I wonder
what part I have played, priest or pander,
to be so ancient-knowing now, and tired.

In Time of Winter

"Hast thou entered into the treasures of the snow?"
The Book of Job

Beyond my rim of sherry small boys
infiltrate, the clatter of sleds, the clink
of skates from shoulders, the shouts, all wooled
and muffled by the new snow like sounds that wink
from the memory. All unwilled,
once more the old dangers, the unearthly joys

arrive. My whole weight imbrutes to wish,
before I know it, that black arctic air
might never blow summer out again.
But I bridle the lunge this side of prayer
thinking of those few molten men
whose one right is blizzard, the full curse and lash.

Somewhere in the wine-warm room is when
I too craved nothing but that the lonely
cold might pounce stinging upon the quick,
when snow across the field was the only
light I had in the dark and thick.

14

Honey Out of Lion

In me the hosts of faith are buried who lived
before me and yet this whited skeleton
is also his. He entered air and grieved
like us and lapsed like us to sticks of bone.

Skulldeep I gaze out still for the cocksure name
and I still trouble the miles with rattle of feet.
But like the people who were there I am
forbidden to demand miracles in the street.

The expert says taking the graves apart
The tooth has lasted longer than the heart.

My jawbones clatter curses with his fame
meaning to pray, and leaves which frenzied weathers
whirl through the autumn hollow all read the same:
let distance be the latest love that tethers

you to him. My chalking arm embraces
a body of fog or snow with an icon heart.
The stone, the skull will not recover faces
while loves are planets and centuries apart.

The witness says whose skill is with the graves
Their teeth have lasted longer than their loves.

Conspiracy

Although you are before time was, the time
has come when you have chosen to reassume
disreputable disguises, a career of crime.

Eternal colloquies murmur in a darkened doorway
and waiters wading through alcoholic gloom
bring with cocktails a scrawled word in the tray.
Men rise and saunter to the upper room.

A man will enter his brother's house and lock
the door, turn off the radio. Then shake
the curtains for microphones, gaze at the clock

and say: If you will come within the hour
to the harlot's attic, recalling the old rumor
grandfather used to hint of, a promised power
that came and hid among us before the terror—

Even upon the scaffold the treason of hope
is offered. A few will know the hangman's lip
is sure to whisper as he adjusts the rope.

Even the torturer between the screams
assures the victim of blood forever wine.
In secret hoarse abbreviated hymns
a chalice troubles the night like a drunken stein.

Small accidental maples beside the road
offer themselves pathetic like children bringing
a gift of dandelions eager and proud.
In exploding skies a few will hear old silence singing.

16

Parked Car

You straightened; your hands flew to your head
tidying your hair, you yawned and shivered;
and, Now I'll have a cigarette, you said.

I lighted up a pair
and by the infant light
I saw you still tidying your hair.

And so we breathed on fires not our own.
Breathed long and hard to stun the blood;
somehow to shock the lung, enflame the bone,
somehow to fetch the body out of stone.

(And as you drank for flame, pale yellow wings
held tremulous war with darkness for your face,
made fluttering reach for your collar's rumpled lace.)

Breath-parched, we tossed the stubs on the night's damp floor
and sat and sat and stared upon
the twin progeny our love could bring to pass:
two mites of fire smoking in the dew
two tiny sun-downs choking in the grass.

Hospital

This bright museum of collected pain
admits its little public at restricted hours:
who bare their heads, take their tip-toe privilege
down antiseptic halls, and afterwards
send books and flowers.

Assorted hurts and notable remains
of life and death, these specimens are laid
neatly in rows, and stacked in storeyed layers.
("Mr. Johns is in Ward eight, third floor.")
The corridor

is bright and hard, and brittle to the feet.
Nostrils detect the sprinkled, prickly-sweet
medicinal holy water casting its spell
against the tiny demon's unseen cell.

Here they are ranged in spotless linen cases;
here you can learn from withered wrists, flushed faces
how desperately the earth has much desire
for rising up and taking foot and walking—
("You must be quiet—the Doctor said no talking!")

Armistice with Doom

"A whole night has passed and it's only Tuesday.
Then we lay bruised where the many bruised lay
and dying where the dying lay. Together
young man and younger wife
we've gone with our loved down Friday's failing weather
where Saturday shuts in the climate of life.

"Is it the shine of Sunday,
a Sabbath setting in dawn,
that lights us back again, no, not to Monday,
but it's only Tuesday, though a whole night's gone."

She now is pale trying to match his word
of what the antennas of their silence stirred
with in both their hemispheres.
But this is woman and soon in joy bolder
than he. Her face sweeps down into his shoulder
where he feels and fears,
how she dares celebrate
the news of the infinite reprieve of fate
at once, hotly, in a champagne of tears.

Survey on the State of the Union

Will you shake hands with a man on a cross?
Click your heels, salute, bow slightly?
Will you commiserate his loss
holding your hat in hand politely?

Would you welcome whole Gethsemanes of grief
that you might show us your rich handkerchief?
A broken shoelace frets you, makes you pause
along your way to being Santa Claus.

Our faith fought for at home and at Tramissene,
our faith prayed for and paid for in the Garden—
(Do you see all polarize to the graph-machine?
Feel the statistics harden.)

Etherized Intelligentsia

The solid labor of the world
sheds gravity, till easy freight
on silk-like caught, up-wafted, whirled,
the universe from one fly dangles
and buzzes toward the height where weight
is lost in pure lines and white triangles.

A cricket crawls down wall to floor,
an antiseptic angel whitely
floats across the corridor—
(Mobility without a flaw
of less or more, here resting lightly
in one unmoving brooding law.)

Here is the staring mind spread thin
and invalid on a bed of space,
remotely relative to skin
envelopment from head to feet,
yet mind without a hand or face—
(No other hands or eyes to meet.)

Even the dim fear cannot increase
that we have slipped above all might
that could restore man-humble peace,
break us to atomic sleep of clods,
could lower or lift us from this height,
this peace of law, not man's not God's.

Lore of the Real

To lie unhearing under rain
and never use the sun,
not like other planted grain
forge wet and hot to one

green shout cracking the burial pause—
this is the allnight doubt
that dims his pillow-nimbus and gnaws
his windowed starglow out.

Till autumn morning urges lore
in slabs of kindling wood.
He grips rough lumber where before
a sign was understood.

Here in his own common garden
he hears the molten nail
hiss through palm and wood, and harden
for his starved sight as braille.

The Chase

The finding in his years of seeking,
the one gift to varieties of prayer,
when trailing hints to many caves
one opened on the radiant lair.

And then he knew the hunter of
this rarest game
was fool, was wild, and the hunted was
the wise and tame.

The mastery of his finding was
that he was found;
the quarry assertive listener, he
the fugitive sound.

His hands came not to fists possessing,
but in warm clasp were gloved;
his triumph like a lover's was,
for he was loved.

The Unhappy Warrior

Father, this child who bayonets cattle,
what of this child,
who ignores the foe but snipes at wind,
snake-beguiled
play-warrior who cannot even find
the field of battle.

Suppose his three hags, like a pressure group,
decree him starved, shot—
will life-fear of dramatic hurt then dim?
What he is not
loads the instant up with doom
when bullets swoop.

But more likely, illusion will teach him till
he's understood
a boy scout science for every crisis
in the wood,
though meeting no direr wildnesses
than his flowerbox sill.

And after stockaded years he'll learn,
but learn very late,
that he has been becoming and is
now his fate,
then scold earless sons about what bridges
are to burn.

Communion

Early in the Eucharist morning
the police are called. Naturally it's murder
one suspects, though more likely last night's
whiskey beating his wife. The routine scourging.
"Are their windshields really bullet-proof?"
she asks. "My dear, I do not know. Shall we
test them?" Laughter.

                    You could roll down your window
though, as you drive past them manning the squad-car
and yell, "That way! That way!" pointing to
the Church, the Mystical Body.

                  "Good morning, Father
Matthews," at the door as you went out.
Full pleasant was his absolution. And handshake.
Now you were clean, ready for breakfast. Seek ye
first the sip and wafer and breakfast shall
be added unto you, I always say.
As well as a fine spring morning. She paused upon
the step a moment to inhale prospects. "Lovely!"
in exhalation.

              But can you blame the police?
Although your mouth be red, not one drop
was spilled on the altar. Bells were heard but who
can testify to cries or even a groan?
All antiseptic as a fair linen cloth.

And Justice is a gentleman, curious
about the cults but never losing perspective.
He puts his questions as if half-joking, yet
not unkindly. He orders the routine scourging
and questions again. Then washes his hands before
the people, showing that he's a tolerant martyr
to the people's wishes.

                    Murder in the Cathedral
shows on Sunday as on other days
and plays to standing room only, Easter and Christmas.

Dogberry and Verges are sophisticated
fellows now and know a play is just
a play. Therefore the squad-car speeds remotely
to where the vintage is being trampled out.

New Age

A brutal quiet threatens through the land.
Its hurricane is furtive in propeller
squalls. You hear it scream from Mother's cupped hand,
Mary, come home. The giant is real, striding
smoke-vague from Tommy's explosion in the cellar.
And all sniff out a funeral blossom hiding
in the incandescent buds that howl through steels.
Noise-icons in temple terminals of wheels
chatter and fume at the last timed roar of all,
and deaf eon stilling down through mouse-squeak and midge-call.

Anecdote of the Wind

The day opened like a story, with a boy
running past the windows. I heard him panting,
I wakened on exclamations in his breathing.
And there was flight in that persistent slanting

along the rows of poplars and in their twinkling
leaves. Last year's leaves like crippled rodents
lunged in the grass. An abstract haste was wrinkling
the taller grass in waves, in waves. Fat clouds

flew steaming. Space stood still, we were the wind,
we, the company of earth. After
the confining dazzle of the sun had thinned
I saw that this same elemental cunning

drove all the worlds and all their hosts to running.

At the Mercy Seat

If this were a city where eyes could find a brush
and hands, I would burnish the city-top
in noon glare. If I could move in this stone hush,
I'd give a daylight even to the bridge.
But on the river, that groping root, I'd drop
such thick and black that no ingenious dredge

could harrow it. Whether found dismembered
or torn with one burnt hole through skin and laces
the woman's body could not be important.
The thing that I had once almost remembered,
almost remembered now, was the only portent.
Gently I explained to the shadows, their faces

staring, and they refused to understand.
There are some dreams dark beyond recall.
When I shouted, the shadows were not unmanned,
for there are dreams that are not dreams at all.

The Hurt of the Second Death

The final mission was the bombing of
the graves. Bombs nearer omega than used
before were needed because neither hate nor love
remained and the dead were deep. There must be springs
to detonate from sheer perception, fused
with the suicide involved in the shapes of things.

The ghosts themselves leaned across the charts
of targets, like shadows of smoke cooling the field
of snow. Jawbones clacking meshed the parts
in planless plans, losses lost. The crew
of ribs, bandaged, belted and annealed,
rose in a hum of distances and flew.

The ejected corpses throw up their long chalk hands
in parabolas of despair.
Once chosen to surrender as much as breath
they've kept the seas and lands,
but there's such trouble now, how can it spare
these bones the second death.

Standard Time, Ithaca

We were long killing the despoilers in
the hall when Elaine crept up behind and said,
I'm sleepy, I'm going on. She fished a pin
from her hair, departing; spoke through pins at the staircase:
turn the thermostat down when you come to bed.

He the lord, you remember, returned disguised
in beggar-skin. If this had not been scarred
as he was, he would have moved unrecognized
through careful and careless memories alike.
That is, until the only door was barred.

Early, I'd left my wife and son in rainbows
of tawny leaf-light and I returned later
with windshield wipers smothering in snows.
My dog scuffled an old shoe of mine through drifts
and knew me, expected it seemed no one greater.

Those suitors prattled indoors and through the town.
"That day," they said, but mostly, "this day, tomorrow."
And as they hinted, yes, Windfinger Hermes
conducts the generations of summer down
leafwise, to rot in the disinfecting snow.

from:

CHILDREN AND OLDER
STRANGERS
1962

Faith on Friday

Never in my innocent unbelieving
days could I have guessed that faith was this
betrayal, this tangled murderous unrelieving
love that ran to light me with a kiss

so all the surrounding darkness might thereafter
know me and probe the old wounds of unbelief.
The angels who should have followed with trump and laughter
came with staves and torches to catch a thief.

I'd waited through my ages like the Jews
to be delivered. Long seasons I would peer
through prayers for prophecies to turn to news
and then whole eras of me would disappear

until disaster and a scrawny sage's word
recalled me to the promise and its labors.
I never once had danced before the lord
of my believing but for my sceptic neighbors

I had often capered. Now the word
had come, not prophets now, but what they'd spoken
of and spoken with. I saw his sword,
I knew it was the faithful would be broken.

The same three ancient crosses mark the hill
where faith meets fate. Stretched on the doubting tree
the flesh of hope is hurt too deep to tell
if I did this to him or he to me.

Food of Love

My dagger struck like a brute
and her flesh parted to the ripe expectant lips
of the kissing wound that she was born with
yet waited for. A speed of light flashed through

our intricate double fuse of nerves,
took our bodies bursting toward heaven
in a mount of fire, and the blade between us
melted in weeping lavas of love, love.

God knows we were joined in the battle,
in our zeal of burning welded of two
God's lonely sex. God knows that love
fell from heaven to our lair of fangs

where the image of soul fragile as breath was torn.
Love taught its bones why bones are always
counted and broken, taught its animal blood
why it must weep its slow dark drops

where the paw pounces and the claws are driven.
O lovers to live must feed on the flesh of love
and drink love's terrible tears. O lovers must taste
their earth breathing the God who is God-forsaken.

Moment in Suburban Summer

Whatever space the anonymous multitudes
of leaves or the named rows of brick
do not inhabit is thick
with the light of noon. Until the dove intrudes.

It's not a song, a cry, or voice. It echoes
merely, revealing hollows
that roll and sound
through the packed air and weave off underground.

And all the streets turn from the crowding sun
to listen down
chasms of unbelief
weighing deep and numb between leaf and leaf.

Departure

From the whiskey-golden nimbus
of the porch light
straight up leaps the immense night.

The ring-around-the rosie glow of us,
the departing guests,
empties up as quick as sight

into the aeons of the dark that rest
around a few crisp stars.
Our little company who divide

unborn from dead majorities creep
along the bottom of the void.
We cross the lawn, stoop into cars,

switch on the lights, briefly warm the motors
and sounding horns to host and hostess at the door
roll rubber-cushioned home, groping for sleep.

Crisis on the Hill

The wild moment shouted with much to hide:
nails to find to hammer down our hands
now strange and tingling with lust to heal and feed
gross crowds with miracles of fish and bread.

Frantic, to search for spikes and so secure
our feet which would persist in walking like clowns
of innocence beside the contagious sinner.
Quick, to imprison our madded heads in crowns

of mockery and send for the pomp of spears
from Caesar's Rome to still the imperious love
ringing in our sides. We could not live
and let our treasury of despairs and fears

be lost which we and our fathers had surely earned.
But still we could not save our losses: our bloody
carcass split the veil in two, the body
of our death stood up in noon and burned

like a torch inside our dungeon of family deeds.
In that eclipse our heaven exposed our horror.
Angels shuddered at our desired monster
and marveled at the light upon our needs.

Vacation Land

A rainy season darkened among the churches
that swung their cross above our speedway. Beaches
were tan on Saturdays and browned our hides,
on Mondays a clean sun rinsed our lake in tides

of sky. But feastdays clouded to a crisis
where damp clothes hung an odor of mouldy spices
down the altar rail. Thunder growled
like poison from swollen clouds, the air blurred cold

the lightning twinkled twinges as of pains
from some imagined crucifixion. Sins
could well have fired the morbid light in which
the Virgin materialized, a hooded witch.

Safe with six days' pagan weather, Venus
laughed each week away with her Adonis
sprawling on foamy sands and leaving glooms
to Christian orgies in the catacombs.

Infidel at the Highest Level

Never was idol-worshipper more subtle.
A living God is needed to catch his tint
of pagan mind. No crudities of metal,
wood or stone betray him to his neighbor,
for his are airy gods sculptured by dint
of thought, his stone a mud of dust which friction
heaps from ego rubbing fact. His labor,
done in public temples, completes his fiction
with imaged Father, Son and Holy Ghost
planted behind his eyes like a totem post.

Never was man more subtle in his dying.
Suppose his static icons spring to light
like atoms bursting, the moment of his going,
to move on majestic stages beyond the air.
His frantic hands will claw against the bright
horizons closing upon him like gates of grief
to clutch those little models of his despair.
But suppose he is perfected in his unbelief.
In the very spasm of his final breath
he'll kick his idols off, seeing death is death.

Pater Noster in Winter

Our prayers have searched his gray horizon for signs
of light unlighted coming, but his will
continues being done by the naked spines
of trees that creak in cold. It is the chill

of twenty centuries that settles on
this moment and stiffens to the look of distance
making our hilltops strange. More has gone
than summer from the face of gardens. His glance

permits the sunny grains we stored in bins
to darken to loaves of stone. This long from heaven
the snow has learned to disinfect our sins.
We sin in crowds, there's no one to be forgiven.

Unless some dear Faust rediscovering hell
and screaming, having outraged all temptation,
might crack the icy distance on heaven's will.
To snatch him, down might pounce our whole salvation.

A Plaint of Flowers

Although, those years, we squandered
grief upon our dead
as rich and wild as blood,
time was the healthy animal

infecting our every breath.
But now, my oldest friend,
expect from me no sorrow
beyond this formal plaint of flowers.

I have no heartbeat moment
left to lavish on any
death but mine. My pride
lies withered here like yours, I feel

your pockets for the penny
you leave behind unspent.
Yet somewhere in this mortician's
scene your death and mine together,

should, like strong young men, stand weeping.

St. Knud's: Sunday within the Octave of the Nativity

"Legend has it that at the moment of Denmark's greatest need the Vikings will rise from the green mounds where they sleep and come forth."

A dust of saints and martyrs obscures the fresh
faces of children in the massive gloom.
The one warm look beams from the hidden lamp
blindly staring up at the infant's crèche.
The priest enters to bells clanging like minor doom
and walks past tongues of Holy Ghost hung damp
above disciples posing in plaster flesh.

The joyful introit issues in a drone.
Lukewarm Kyrie Eleisons must leave
the Heart of Love a statue nine times dumb.
We celebrate the Gloria in mechanic moan
and now that the Child of Triumph has clearly come

exultant Alleluias seem to grieve
our voices slightly from the one indifferent tone.
The priest ascends the pulpit, an electric switch
lights up the broken body of the Word.
The live voice flickers across the feeble silence
where St. Paul preaches memories from his niche.
After Amen, the heroes who have not heard
oppress us with crowds of absence before the Presence:
The poor Magdalenes, the Josephs among the rich

not here to anoint the Body in spice or tears.
But now like thunder approving the Elevation
a truck outside rises on crescendos of gears
above the lesser traffic in exultation.
The absence fills the pews, there is no lack.
The weak are here until the strong come back.

Peter and John Running

First is the woman, almost falling, panting
out the news of the ponderous door standing
ajar. And then the dreamy Sabbath of grief
that they have drowsed in, splinters into life.
Why have they stayed together near the scene?
The play was over Friday, the audience gone.
In this cruel moment of waking to premonition

begins the strangest race that was ever run.
For both are victors before their legs begin
and running for life they run straight toward the dead.
He who is named beloved flies with the speed
of innocence and wins because the feet
of the other one are bruised with fatigue of guilt.
Yet now you see the loved one hesitate

at the deadly door. Winning more future than he
can cope with he has to throw his laurel away.
Shy and delicate as a maid while he stoops
hoping to see and not see, the other leaps
with all the crude weight of his need into the tomb
and so wins all he lost. Where he the lame
has blundered a passage, though, the fleet can come

as well. He enters and stands, simply watching
with the wide soft eyes of a child the other snatching
among the linens and the napkin as if
he searched for what he's buried, behind a thief
whose theft enriched. For here are both their graves:
if no dear flesh is found, they find their lives.
Before there is belief, the loved believes.

Last Things

I

The blow that felled him left my father's one
hard hand lying as limp as a cast-off glove
of leather. Now it was for me the son,
by a logic that overwhelmed us both, to shave
his harsh old face each day he had to live.
Revulsive my fingers explored the abyss of love

we'd carefully kept between us, and touched as tender
a skin as a baby girl's. A pain of wonder
struck and flashed among the ages lost
in silent accumulations behind my back.
My ignorant fingers sparkled with the cost
he'd paid for anger vigilant to attack,

not sparing wife and child who could hurt the most.
In the city of friends, so subtle was their approach,
he'd had to erect the barricades of reproach.
Yet for all his rage, with a shield as thin as his
I admired the luck he'd needed in having lost
only a hand, war being what it is.

II

There came the last day of my father's breathing
when there was nothing, nothing to do except
to suffer time which suffered to a close.
I stared across his bed with rage seething
through me at how the trees he'd planted slept
outside our window permitting the fact of snows

to settle cold upon them and around
them. Stupid they stood while the ashes of desolation,
falling, reached and never reached the ground.
Anger as thick as blood was my consolation
for the storm of silence bleaching breath and space
since nothing strong and tall out there had grace

enough to toss defiance or even to bend
before this beginning of memory and its end.

The Improvement of Prayer

I prayed the little words like children's games
safe and secret from terminals and streets.
I played the shiny imaginary names
like toys, hiding delight from solemn speeds
and powers, from the tall buildings and adult noise.

I spoke a star, a baby God, a stable.
I whispered haloes in oxen-eye and straw.
Repentant, I indulged my vice of fable
with crucifix and beads, I counted the row
of saints and martyrs in parables of creeds.

Then as if a child picked up a seed
and found that he's uprooted a universe,
I heard my secret splitting with public speed
through husks of noise, I saw my words swing doors
and leave the grown-up streets little with toys.

Childhood Scene Revisiting

The light of eye, the tuning ear refuse
the tale that windshield, windows, and common wheels
unroll. The opaque presence of self and steel
in this pure village of geometric hues

is miracle too sheer. And yet these tires
arouse real dust. It smokes across designs
of roofs and rooms where history endures
thin allegories of mumps and measles. Lines

turn the trees where abstract apples hung
forbidden. The shrunk dimension is what appalls.
It is true, then, a boy can grow so tall
his epic dwindles to this brief plot of song.

Meanwhile the boy chagrined is thumping your face
and chest with knuckles he knows are impotent.
"I never lived in any solid place,"
he screams. Truism where a lie is meant.

Sweet Killer

All day I took my time and eased along
the parks, through restaurants, department stores
and bars. All the sunny day I felt
the lead jump in my coat, tug my shoulder.
My load is light, my weight is but the lilt
of wisping boys and girls in revolving doors.
I reel my tune in a simple metal folder.

I paid the driver his dollar, added a nickel
for his insolence. I gave him his hour
laughing because I felt the cold thing tickle
me, and I was little David, the power
of blushing pebbles had made me sweet and fickle.

My load is light, aching sweet my sorrow.
Listen, street-hammers, to my lullaby.
Now all these people walked today, tomorrow
how different they may be if some will die.

The cashier there with her old-fashioned locket
between high breasts was not so terribly strong
as once. I fondled the trigger in my pocket,
my hand on her little penny-bank where she
was saving for her hero to come along.
I talked with her and laughed, it was a song
to have her where all the people could come and see.

My eyes are blue-eyed Jack. If I tumble down
the slope, I keep my pocket and there's the lump
of my importance that drags down brown-eyed Jill.
Down she falls, her high breasts go bump, bump.
Not in fairy tales but in this town
I am the hero of my own sweet will.

I had my leisure knowing as I walked
that I could hiss my horn for zany BoPeep.
I stood and grinned whenever stoplights balked
my way. I gazed at all my street of sheep.

There at the crossroads of public dreamy noise
I hid my thumb and rubbed it across the barrel
of jukebox tunes that unborn girls and boys
will wriggle to, when sound is quick and sterile.

I have the secret that will nudge and reach
the coyest selves under the thump of blood,
will peel them down to bare of bone, and teach
them love is perfect only in that nude.

On the Adoption of Sons:
An Anniversary

I stand and watch them, feeling awkward and glad
like any supernumerary Joseph.
They both are kneeling, the woman and the child,
their heads together. The closed window makes me deaf

but I can see them talking over the bud
or bug in the summer grass. I watch and love her
for the son I love but never gave her.
She carried him in her prophetic blood

through ages. And I too suffered the love she suffered
for all the children in all the strangers' houses.
I ached with her meek envy of the mothered
world. And still the little outcast Moses

lay hidden until one day our telephone
rang bells from a distant city and sudden flesh
was made of abstract faith. There we shone
with alarming haloes, standing inside the crèche

and trembling before the baby whose large brown eyes
accused our ignorance of what he understood.
We saw and marvelled how fingers of this toy-size
could bless all children with crosses of brotherhood.

Our lilting Ford escaped the city of signs
and fearful joys, and swung him with us home
to Nazareth. But always, always shines
in our known street and house that Bethlehem.

Of course this story, our story, is travesty
and passers-by may joke in fun or guile.
But when we look at them, the authentic three,
they are not laughing, not frowning; we see them smile.

Child

He lives where everything is heavy and tall.
Either the world won't budge or it threatens to fall
upon his head. His father's house can reel
with fright, the doors and stairways make a fool
and dwarf of him. His glass of milk is full
before it's filled, the tops of desk and table
submerge his inches to his chin. A fable
ia all that makes him a policeman or able
to drive a speedboat and to lasso cattle.

When, in public, he turns his somersault,
some chair or sofa lurks with bump and insult.
He must be lifted to taste the cool white fountains.
His arms must concede his father can carry mountains.
His miniature nerves cannot lift and use
the worn shapes of hates and loves without a bruise.
Wherever he tumbles or splashes, wherever he runs
his heritage stares down on him in tons.
Sometimes his joy is great—he laughs and leaps—
and sometimes he sorrows until he falls asleep.

Toy Windmill

Together we whittled a stick of sunny
afternoon and made
the wind something we could see.
Partly it was sad
and scary seeing the gashes but funny
too seeing the knife sliver neatly.

I shaved the wavy sunlight off
but you had harder work
watching until we planted our staff
and the limp wood unfurled with a jerk
and began to spin out a stiff
noise like a joke and you could laugh.

The wind will tumble your blocks all down
today or tomorrow. But once
you heard above the roses a clown
flutter and rattle, you laughed at a dunce
of wood, and you will own
this secret even when the blowing makes your boats all drown.

Girl Three Years into the World

The love half-dreaming through me feels like laughter
merely because she's so much smaller, warmer, softer,
sleeping along my side, than any bosom lover

I've had or could have had. Her knuckles dimple
in parodies of women's hands, her face a simple
little stratagem of health before the ample

mind of beauty ripens. Let God have praise
for loaning me this love of her that laughs and plays
in the dozing silence of moments before the sun's full rise

to balance my other love of her, its twin
who for her sake grieves all day for the world she's in
dark with calamity and the evil made by children of men.

Bus to Marienlund

The blind man sat beside his
wife and each one held a great-eyed
blue-eyed child and each child held a
crowd of flowers that gazed out wide and
glad.

The bright day went a deeper bright, the
people on the bus looked right at
this father and this mother and
then they flicked their sight on
one another.

Chair with Rockers

It's all that two years old can do,
plying those rubber muscles, to lever
up her body, then so to sit
as to hold the equilibrium true

while the grave old rockers tilt and groan.
But deaf to this defective pitch
of age she alarms me to resent
how recklessly she sways her throne.

I never saw grandfather ride
that same old hobbyhorse of time
but glimpsed enough in tintype whiskers,
his small son upright at his side.

Him, my father, I do recall,
his flesh gone thin and stiff as bone,
working this chair like a pendulum.
Shrunk close to elemental skull

his head wobbled across the innocence
he'd spent, long Sunday afternoons,
reading newspapers which stilled his rocking
to sweet forevers of arrogance.

All have staged their parts, my own
is merely to attend this moment
which here imposes our insolence
even upon a child's soft bones.

I labor to hold our ritual true
against all pity for small gay figures
lilting on saddles of old presumption.
But despite what fifty years can do

love shrivels helplessly to knees
before her, and ineffective arms
would keep her squirming body, she laughing
half in proud protest, half in glee.

Subway Train

Huddled flights of hands clutch at gleams
of rods and leathers,
free adjust to floors
that tilt like dreams,
and eyes become a single window blurred.
These hypnotic postures
prove that love's too humble and absurd
ever to be defied
by mere hand and head.
They cannot drop the toy that love conjures
up from caves of speed.

Remember how tendrils of the pumpkin vine
desiring the stalks of corn
seized instead the shine
of a child's horn
and tangled the orphan metal in with life.
Despite all green they lost,
the tender fingers—their love still big in leaf—
seemed proud to turn to rust.

Day In, Day Out

The day is but a ritual that keeps
the heaven of the future streaming
through his muscles, and when he sleeps
it's only from fatigue of dreaming.

There follows an agony of nights,
sick-green, corrupt with youth. Pillows
swell with sweetness, fleshing with whites
of breast and thigh among wet shadows.

By day the air he breathes is loud
with heroes. The prince or seer that he
must soon become calls from a cloud
and each hour is drenched in destiny.

At last that dry noon rises which dulls
the brightness no aftertime redeems.
He looks behind him: dead men's skulls
are dreaming his sad diminished dreams.

Once the raw husk is dried and shed
he stands in vision the dreamer lacked.
The unknown stares from the day ahead
as terrible and beautiful as fact.

Surgery Ward, December 8

Relieved by prayers or years from such erratic
terrors as toss the young through their ecstatic
waste of soul, my nerves secure upon
the firm old substance of human dread, I go
down, then, in sleep before him, toward the still zero.

Many of my townsmen weep, not for sin
but cold, this morning, stumbling through stiff snow
in air where doors stick and motors refuse to spin.

Sinking to my encounter under thought
I hope that bones and muscles may remember
during the mock-eternity of numbed hours
to use such holds as habit should have taught
of faith and love before his strength dismember

me. Snow falling deep on fallen cold
endows with immaculate body this December
day. Here time lies hiding in sheeted folds

until the logic of mindless flesh in trouble
begins to lift, slow bubble after bubble
bursting absurd on the walled pastels of noon.
White figures interrupting with other prisms
of touch, pour rainbows of stinging drowsy chrisms.

The boy dawdled in this day's whited womb
tonight wrings back to birth the mechanisms
of toes and fingers in the anguish of heated rooms.

Now the crisp waking of the eyes in dark
aloneness, the familiar world of hours recovered
whole. A television tower reddens
the window like a heart, its pulsing spark
keeping time to old flesh rediscovered.

Although I go back to my people lame
the skillful wound he gave will heal. And those
glad in their love to see this face the same
as they've seen change with years, cannot suppose
I come among them blessed with a new name.

Portraits

The young inhabit souls but lightly
haunted by their fathers' flesh.
They move in bodies resembling sprightly

shadows through which all hurt and pleasure
diffuse to instant torsions of hate
or ecstasy. Leaping they measure

an expedition by the spirit,
unaware there lurks in nerve
and bone a weariness to fear it.

Then sad to watch them slowly turning
into bodies when bodies least
become them. When most they should be burning

ghosts, they sit there not reflecting
on realms ethereal, only yearning
for muscles brightly resurrecting.

Anti-Drama

I'd just awakened from the villains and heroes
that dream down time forever, I'd pushed away
my bed of noble Rolands and wicked Neroes
when he peered through my window in his ominous way.

Blinking my eyes I thought the melodrama
was true, after all, and I was to be the victim
sprawling before the shabby cyclorama
to start the plot and inspire the wit and vim

of the live actors. But all the weapon he had
lurked in his eyes and this he walked away
with before it could penetrate my bony head.
The only power he used was day after day

to reappear with the same incomplete surprise
which left me nothing to confide to police
or friends. For there was nothing to surmise
from his accusing, weakly pitying face.

He startled sorrows, his sudden gaze would loom
like a far-off light of laughter upon a grief.
His eyes would sting a holiday with doom
or etch a comedy in sad relief.

Last night my words could see what I'd observed
for months, as he stared in and moved away
as usual. How long, I wondered, has this youth served
me? My God, I said, already his hair is gray.

The Change of Seasons

At first the seasons took up names
from language scuffled out by boys.
Green field and snow hill signaled toys,
weather was nothing but changing games.

The boy grown lover christened spring.
Green with acres of budding breath
he rode on safe rich moods of death
as if to contemplate such sting

of love's release, the wound in flood
would drain his whole man's life away.
But love endured to show a day
of blue-cold snow inflaming blood.

In time love found its labor, games
went idle and passions passed their toys
to other lovers and later boys.
Still the seasons kept sweet names.

But old ambiguous pain was trite
last spring and these blank heaps of December
cold mark nothing to remember.
All seasons tick away the light

of time itself, a brittle din
of hearts whose love is not quite done.
The year emerges a skeleton,
the abstract drama closes in.

L'Après-Midi d'un Homme

In afternoon as if in morning
he surprises the nude
of day. It gives no warning
that he has blundered back to the crude

riot of dawn. The violent gift
that swells the scene
almost smothers him with a spendthrift
lust and pride of green on green.

He reels in despair if he must count
the squandered grasses,
the spending of stems and leaves that mount
the four directions of hills in masses,

if he must plumb the lake, the soul
that meditates
at the womb of this profusion and makes whole
the luxuriance of generations in one date,

drinking the trees around its rim,
inverted, down
into its heart where deep clouds swim
indifferently through skies that drown.

His gazing fails at the bold expense
of light that pours
on minute after minute immense
accumulations in eras of stars.

He puzzles how to move and take
the exorbitant moment,
the Now that shines in leaves and lake,
with only hands for instrument.

His thick words fumble what yes to say
that he may press
lips and loins against the day
and so with grateful passion possess,

and fathom time as for thanksgiving,
raw grasp on good
deferred, a ritual long as living
not being too long for gratitude.

Late afternoon he understands,
morning behind
him, how touch must be through rites of hands
and sights through the formal dark of mind.

In the very substance of the lake
he dips his bony
fingers, knowing they lift to slake
his thirst with nothing but ceremony.

Kite Umbilicus

A moon wet with rainbow ring cannot illumine
cause for wind to crackle like an omen
in one leafless tree till you recall the boy
whose kite drowned yesterday in a branch of sky.

No need for condescending to his dismay
but look for him leading his mates tomorrow
from flying ages beyond what you and moon
have spent your joined and separate light upon.

You see your son among them, his words and gestures
estranged by a second fathering far from yours.
In that compassionate gaze of his you feel
him measure your earthy politics of soul.

Their pity speeds with violence, flings you up
until the cord that feeds and tugs you snaps.
Where they begin breathing their very lives
you gasp on distance which suffocates your loves

and down they plunge with you, drowning in the tree.
There winds erode your warning against the sky
to bare crossbones of kite which even the earthbound
moon forgets, circling around, around.

News Item: Chimpanzee Escapes from Zoo in Antwerp

In Antwerp where as everywhere they blink
skyward through imaginations dark with the speed
of engineered angels, the people shrink
before the apparition of chimpanzee
strutting frankly along the street. In a glee
of danger they breathe-in the hot hairy stink
of equatorial terror like freshened air.

Of course they run, for being just as far
advanced in fright as all of us now are
only an unsophisticated scare
like this can hurt them or draw blood from the abstract scar
winding like a fuse around their marrow.
The chimpanzee, however, at large to stare
for once at worlds that stared at him runs amok.

A caricature of prophetic weathercock,
you might say, he swings his body in sacred rage
up to the jungle of housetops and begins to tear
historic tiles and stones apart, age by age.
Therefore to end the story he must be shot
and the whole fairy tale becomes the kind of joke
you wonder if you should tell the children or not.

Whan That Aprille, Etcetera

Here is the sun, nothing but explosion,
exuding light to hide in, soft as shadow,
and sweetly warming the tongues of the wind's erosion
to lick away the trivial April snow.

Waking in nudes of dreams where nothing but news
in sheerest algebras occurred all night,
we quickly dress to meet the springtime views
spread thick like old prints along the public street.

Our nighteyes blinking to watch shrubs unfold
their walls along the sidewalks in ordered curves
can see nothing but seething suns. The old
indolent leafing is triggered now on nerves

of sleep stretched to the torment of all we know.
Houses in their rows poise like gases
on abstract lawns. Under the failing snow
fuses wait in a billion violent grasses.

Before noon strikes, nothing is left but spring
and as we cross the street archaic-legged,
bare concrete particles set our feet to tingling.
We cringe across on shells immensely egged,

and yet the future fossiling at our bone
has not erupted. It's strange how strange it seems
that streets of twigs budding with wings have gone
right on sleeping through our real dreams.

Salutation

On this day, four years from my daughter's birth,
with our antennas spread alert for good wishes,
in flies a pheasant with a message worth
attention, it seems, if only because she crashes

blind against the house breaking her neck
and doing clumsy winged somersaults to the ground.
Statistics of our awe resist this wreck
of feathers which we stand awkwardly around,

for both the grown-ups and the children at the party
refuse to read this twitching omen, feeling
it's much too primitive for us and vaguely dirty
though one child, to get a closer look, is kneeling.

We do not ask the neighbors, who take the bird
home for dinner, if they'll observe details
which are unusual or even if they've heard
of the interest Homer had in the lay of entrails.

My son selects two feathers for his wall
and pins them among his banners like crossed arrows.
Besides the pheasant, we've seen a cardinal
this spring and a few robins among the starlings and sparrows.

Logos

Words are all the life our mute machines
can have, their only thought in mindlessness.
The rich go begging through slums in limousines
for some poor word to unlock their helplessness.

The wise cry out in the market place for humble
proverbs to ease their pained aridities.
Poets go blind with silence, dancers stumble
against their own unnamed rigidities.

The poor and meek when they've accosted stand
bewildered and turn their moving picture hearts
inside out like pockets. They show their mind
of television wisdom and neon arts

freely, dumbly, never once suspecting
the crimes of everyone they thus confess.
Once more, elect and crowd are waiting, expecting
new words to flourish from the wilderness.

Yet wordless terror pleading in grammar of noise
perceives no omen that will not flash and roar.
It may be none will hear the sad still voice
when ships are drowning and fire is at every door.

The Word and the Fish

If winds that shake the world with air
drove with water, the din would be
too loud by tons for bones to hear,
too blurred with chaos for words to see.

At seaside the world of speech and bone
turns to the teeth that rip its edges
or turns once more and knows its own
flood crashing on the shifting ledges.

Whatever growling miles have been
and are, whatever roar from stone,
only in this frail scaleless skin
are the pride and terror of seas known.

On this escaping fish depend
whatever fates old waters keep:
if thundering up to a sleepless end
or drowning down to shapeless sleep.

Poète Manqué

I have beaten him often, head and heel
says the Lord, and I find no sound in him,
neither the savage growl of the drum
nor the sweet clean resonance of the bell.
I never hear the sea of the seasons roll
through him, nor night and day toss and hum.
A sodden gourd, or cracked vessel, says the Lord,
he is good for nothing now but heaven or hell.

LIKE ANY ROAD ANYWHERE
1976

The Poem Out on a Night Mission

He stands in the abrupt night
of her door, the poem standing
beside him, anxious. With erect
fist he pounds at her wooden
body. Open up, you bitch,
my love, damn you, open
yourself up, you sweet bitch.
(What language for a lover,
grumbles the poem, shivering.)

I've become all instrument,
I'm my only weapon, I've made
myself all key to push myself
whole into your lock, I'll make
you all lock, I'll unlock you.

Faintly the door swings
from its frame (like thighs
spreading, the poem thinks,
remembering her bed the day before).

I have a guest. Won't you come in
and meet him? Slowly he enters
her body with the other man.
The blood of his fist sinks.

Love is a telephone receiver
wrenched off its hook, it drains
drop by drop into an all-night
busy signal.

           The poem
disappears behind everything.
Gathering the light of half-moon
and a few stars into its mind
it creates the city end to end.

Across the street there's a weighty matron
looks out her window. What a beautiful
night, she almost whispers, troubled
by an old magic. Of course it's beautiful,
the poem says, but who can know,
if I don't, what it's made of?

The Poem Dresses Up like Love

The poem contrives to look as old
as love itself, Sappho in Merlin's white beard.
It questions the glum lover: So how did
your story end? I told her I was leaving her.
I couldn't tell her I knew she was leaving
me for her new lover. Your pride, was it?
(Stroking the beard) My pride, yes. And besides
I didn't want her to hurt, even a little.

You ungrateful egotist, mutters the venerable
poem, you could have left her a small gift
of her guilt. What if she wants to remember you?

The Poem as a Private Persecutor

Despair, the poem says to its victim,
was what you wanted from the start.
You wanted the toy, the cloth animal
you'd fondled from childhood to turn
real. You wanted a real lover now
who could enter you live and lash
your blood till your haven of bone
shattered to fragments.

And of course, the poem pontificates,
you found her. She was there
when you looked. (I helped you look.)
Destiny, poem wagging a finger, is nothing
but what your whole life asks for.

Go straight to hell, thinks the victim,
and turns a bare back to the poem
though not so abruptly as to risk whipping.

The Poem as Baby-Sitter

I

Her father kisses her cheek,
then slams the car door shut
and the dim light over her head is quenched.
Kiss and dark feel the same to her,
they close her in, alone,
outside her father's voluminous night.

Only the poem stays with her.
The poem, she thinks, is comic books
piled in the back seat.
It's too dark now to read them.

She hears her father's shadow
walking fast on concrete whispers to the house.
She watches. The door blinks open,
stares, winks shut. And father
has disappeared into a woman
standing tall in a blonde moment of light.

Her housecoat was red, the child
records as for a picture not yet composed.
The poem will remember.

II

How willful a girl-child is
who is told to wait. She'll march
on the small feet of her aloneness
toward any forbidden house. And the poem,
the sad reluctant poem, will guide her
to the bedroom window because it must.

The slit in the furry curtain is narrow
but wide enough for a poem's eye of a child.

At first all she sees is tossing nakedness,
a mad comic book not read before,
all men and women in the world naked.
And then wild pictures focus clear to father
wrestling the woman, he pins her
to her bed, flat on her back,
she writhes under him, eyes closed.

The poem hears its girl-child listen
to older brothers as far away as home
cheering for Dad, waving their muscles.

Night air goes sick as fumes,
she gags, trying to breathe,
and the poem huddles her back to the car.
She waits there for her father's wheels
to hurry the whole earth forward.

She shivers, the poem warms her with silence,
it hears her scramble among her selves,
knocking things over.
She's looking for what she barely knows,
like a rumor indistinctly heard on school playgrounds.

She whispers to the poem as to a self:
He's making me again, isn't he,
inside a woman who is not my mother.
Tomorrow I must choose to be reborn
out of the woman's or my mother's strangeness.

Survival against the Poem

The poem sits on the same chair
as the lover. They look like one.
The lover and his love are saying
their last goodbyes by telephone.
Their poem dwindles to lone words,
to whispers, to silence. Reaching out
as for a last caress the lover
lowers the telephone handset gently
down on its bed. It clicks in place
like a heavy lock no one has a key to.

The poem melts from him through the wall.
Outside, it flies up on black wings,
it rests on the telephone line still warm
with the old, the long goodbye of lovers.

The lover can't move in his chair.
Like a shattered web of wires his nerves
let go of him, they let him drop down
the unplumbed hole inside his skin.
Here where belly and guts are blind
animals that jostle him in the dark
and the wet mouths of heart and lungs
softly nuzzle him, he snuggles warm.
Below despair is safer than above.

So sit there on your telephone wire,
old blackbird of a poem, your claws
tingling with the long farewell of lovers.

The lover won't move for you, won't tempt
destruction by a single twitch of thought.
He waits and slowly begins to change
into an ugly, shapeless thing
whose stench rises from a million years
in the sea. He crawls on feeble fin-legs
onto land, into air, he breathes pain
like lightning flashing back at the sun.
Sprawled on his rock he celebrates
as dimly, as dumbly as glands the breathing
that is in him, the thump of blood.

So tickle your toes, dark ode of a bird,
with the sad electric glow of love's long ending.
Ages below you the lover lives.
He grins in the dark like some misshapen fish.

Her Poem

I

The poem is all hers. It begins
with questions: how did she arrive
at this strange place that for thirty
years had always looked like home?

Is her affliction a disease long
undetected or a sudden wound?
She grows thin, sleeps little, her eyes
darken to see ghosts everywhere.

She becomes her own desperate detective,
searching out his car, empty
and still as death, in the woman's driveway.
(No ghost, this, the poem concedes.)

II

Her door cheeps open like a bird
troubled in its nest. He is home.
His false kiss betrays in her a mob
of armed agonies she never knew were there.

This man whose grazing sleeve was enough
to cure all ills goes numb as ice.
Priests of her soul sit hunched around her,
hands on knees like limp clichés.

In the same instant she and the poem
understand: only this Judas,
this familiar stranger, can heal her now.
The one lover she needs is her betrayer.

III

The poem lowers her in a pool of sleep
and there her love is squeezed from her flesh
in a chain of pointed stones. Where
is her Iscariot? Will he kiss her blood?

Winter dawdles. Will spring ever come?
she asks the poem, waking. Will spring
bring back nothing but this: at midday
a mock lover reeling with moonlight?

IV

The earth rolls over on its back
inviting love. The poem points to where
her lover comes weighted with his flagon
of repentant wine. He pours it over

her nakedness, brow to toe, gently,
like one expensive caress without
a seam. Her silk of woman skin
drinks dry his art of hands, of lips.

(An art new-learned of the other woman?)
Hush, the poem whispers. It will
teach her how to wash the blood
from his wine, slowly, kiss by kiss.

Around his head and loins she feels
tingling halos of the absolution
which her body begs her to give.
But love yearns faster than heart can beat to.

V

The priestess cries out from her suffocating
confessional of tears: you're not yet clean
of me. Forgive my incomplete forgiveness
until my clotted spirit drains and heals.

The poem nods to her imperfect
lover who now takes her, shivering,
into his arms. Nightlong he holds
her warm, the poem keeping watch.

The Poem Is Showing

Slowly, without embarrassment,
the poem composes the candles on the sideboard
to show how mortal our hands are,
putting down or picking up a glass,
fingering among the hors d'oeuvres,
or touching a friend's shoulder.

In the twilight of table lamps
and floor lamps which the poem invents
for the next room, how sadly
our skeletons show through
as we stand or sit, conversing
with a certain animation.

Poem by Movie Camera

I

The poem enters your head, takes over your eyes.
You're still yourself, yet now you're the poem's dream
of you. You see, but you don't control the muscles
of your seeing. Else why would you be scanning,
back and forth, the green rug at your feet?
What could you expect to find? Until your gaze
is fixed for you on a brown oak leaf that punctuates
the green current of the floor. Is it a question,
a statement, a command?

              The poem that dreams
your eyes pulls you near. You must obey, you kneel
and the leaf grows larger, larger, filling all you see.
It lies deep in the rug like the fossil footprint
of an animal long extinct.

              The soundtrack
picks up the mellow scuff of footsteps coming close.
And there before you, before the leaf, two soft leather
slippers halt. The camera tilts your eyes up,
slowly, to absorb the figure of a man, inch by inch,
in pyjamas and dressing robe. His hair flows white,
his back is slightly bent, he shoulders slightly stooped.
He's looking down. (But he can't see you of course.
He's real, you're the dream, remember?)

He stoops and from the microphone inside him
you hear the rasp of joints, the thudding swim
of blood to brain. You see a hand of dry skin
and knotted knuckles claw the leaf up like a harvest.

You watch him straighten. He shuffles toward a desk
in the dim corner. In a brief ritual of hands
he crumbles the leaf like fire crackling into an ashtray.

He talks to himself. (He doesn't know you're here, remember?)
He tells himself, It's the one thing I've done today,
picking up an oak-leaf, November-brown,
and so I keep my green floor clear.

II

I wish, the poem says, I could give you
eyes and ears three centuries back.
Because imagine him sitting there
in an upper room of a public house
or in a room next to the stage, actors
pushing in and out to put on costumes, faces.
You hear his quill plop in ink,
jerk across the page in staccato scratches.
A dream-world of queens and wenches,
kings and clowns, flutters down to you
on the feather waving in his fingers.

He's just finished his tragedy of a man
gone wild with the pride of age and grief.
It's all I've done this day, he tells himself,
revising a dozen lines. And I wish you may expire
with every word, you withered bull's pizzle.
(He's thinking of the ancient who plays the king
and has complained about his speeches in the death scene.)

III

It's almost a year later the poem dreams you
again, outdoors at night. You see the camera crew
busy as ghosts under stars that are millions of years
ago. A telescopic lens becomes your eye,
sweeping the milky way, slowly, back and forth.
The crowd of stars leap clear but among them all
not a wisping memory of a man who picks a leaf up
off a floor, who revises a play, who rages in a storm.

The poem's pictures, you protest, fall out from machines
of eyeballs, nerves and brain. They point you to the wrong places.
But you're inside the poem, inside yourself.
You can see. You can even see how far old men and young
can go and where the poem and old and young men end.
You can see, you're inside. In slow motion
you breathe into yourself that indifferent joy
you've always wanted to love with.
You bless the poem with both hands.
Your blessing beams out in all directions.

Sleeping on Down

Sleeping as you do in a basement
with a sleeping dog is already,
the poem argues, a downward
joining toward origins, a slippage.

To sleep with the fish that are suspended
in the ocean would be a deeper drowning,
and how near the zero of creation
sinks the limp dream the seaweed
is tangled in?

                So be careful,
the poem warns, where you begin
to sleep your nights down from,
especially if your finny fingers
itch to write of such decremental
linkages. After all, says the poem,
I have myself to think of.

The Poem Takes a Walk

The greatest thinker of the age walks in the middle.
My father walks on the other side of him.
I'm nearest you, moving in the poem, watching
for you with the poem's eyes.

                                      I've forgotten the great man's
name but it doesn't matter, he's known to everyone. He walks
unmindful of his innocence as if strangers had hastily bought
his expensive clothes and flung them around him.

                                      Although
my father keeps precisely abreast, it's *his* stride,
easy and bouncy, that leads. His right arm, swinging,
swings the wise man's left, like two arms linked in handcuffs.

I can't believe how freely my father swings
his left hand too, a two-pronged hook of steel,
the weapon which wounded every day of my boyhood
but which he used to hide in his pocket whenever
strangers came to our elm-shaded, half-opened door.

The street we march down feels like the natural dark
between night and morning stretched out unnaturally long.
A few huddled, faceless figures, groping singly, in pairs,
in small groups, must do for people. Occasional cars
float by, glare-eyed blind, rubber-deaf. Streetlamps
fumble the clear air as if lighted by fog.

Dirt farmer, and janitor at last, my father
could not remember which April he quit the one-room school
on the hill where all the twenty pupils ciphered
and read from the same two books year after year.

Now he and the man of wisdom walk together
in bland assurance. I stumble trying to keep in step
with them, my father's left foot timed to the great man's
right. Is it a dance they both were born with?
Or have they rehearsed it many times in a secret place?
I who am known by my father's walk never knew my father.

Maybe where he's been dead for thirty years
my father has learned where he must marshal
the wise man of the age. Is it exile, escape,
a public ceremony to honor him, prison, execution?

Don't be so anxious, the poem said, or you'll wake me up
before we get there. But how could I help it? Because
we kept on walking, walking, to my father's
jouncing stride, till I had recognized the movement,
could feel the rhythm of bedded lovers rising in me,
rising, I couldn't stop it, and here I am,
alone, wet with the riddle of the old realities.

Revisiting the Confessional
as a Tourist

This is the place I used to lug my sins to
as if I carried the weight of my own absence.
The void was only a few holes then
but heavy enough already.

In whispers he told me to pray yet the poem heard him.
How could I help praying? After all, I began
bowed to my knees in the waters of the womb.

Rebaptizing Father, wash the death-smell
of your withering genitals off your fingers
and water me in the font of my own sorrow.
Then see how you make me grow.

I remember the poem told me: the real dark
is a door you can walk through
but can never open.

Outside, the wind whimpered like a beggar
asking no less of me than a life.
The poem stood so still it almost disappeared.

Sometimes, sleeping among the brutes,
I seem to remember when brain turned into mind
and the gods were born.

Poem Almost in Time for Easter
(For John Matthias)

"Yesterday a man identified as Timothy Eastman was found stabbed to death in his apartment at 324 Lamont Avenue."
From a newspaper story,
Saturday, March 29, 1975

The poem arranged it for him. How else
could he be murdered on the very Friday
which has for centuries been called good?

For instance he hardly noticed that the door
he'd left behind him locked was now unlocked.
Yet the betrayer who stood inside in the shadows,
close enough for a friend's embrace, he knew at once.

He even recognized the knife, it glittered
with the sunlight of his mother's kitchen, it had
carved for years the warm meat of his birth.

The potted lily slipped from his hands,
he heard its roots suck at the floor.
The stab however was too sudden, he could not
believe until he'd stuck his hand in the wound.

Not in the flash that ripped the holy curtain
but in the darker light of thunder that lingered
on, he saw forming the one chance in his sixty years
to cry out, Nothing is finished! Nothing!

But then, as if to keep the secret, the poem
left his voice, and not even his patriarchs
came running from their graves to speak for him.

And so he knew it was he alone who was
surrendering, as each living thing at last
surrenders and no one is to blame.

It was he skulking down out of himself
by the back stairs, his legs melting, and he
seeping into the spring rain outside.

There, in blood as bland as water, he'll rinse
the soft bones of snow from street and avenue
to make way for saviors marching with their saints
and for demons pranking with their sinners.

The Poem Fails at Michel's, Hairstyling for Men

"But the very hairs of your head are all numbered."

The poem holds open the door to this parlor
of sorcery. You enter but protest at once
that all the magic has been scraped off.

The perfumes tainting the air are tinsel
ghosts, they could kill acres of flowers.
Bare numbers that have counted lives over
and over in those cushioned chairs in a row
spring up, clanking, in the cash register
like mounted skeletons.

But see, the poem insists, that man
sitting still as death in his high seat,
the mystic robe draped over his shoulders,
arms and lap. Watch him shut
his eyes, open them, stare dazed
at the empty space around his feet,
then close them again. Under the spell
of the shaman who stands beside him anointing
his head, the man dozes toward vistas.

Understand, it's the hair of the man's head
the medium is stirring his hands in,
it's a man's head, it's where nerves have gathered
from rock and leaf, from fish, bird and reptile,
all come home at last to play
sad, comic games.

And look—the poem points—that ring
on the necromancer's finger, weaving
in and out of the trance. It's flashing
signals toward a future here
already in the mirror. From his side
of the dream the man has not yet seen it
or he would seize the hand and kiss
the ring's meaning. But maybe he does see,
maybe he's hissing through the teeth
of his bowed head: kill, kill that serpent
coiled around your finger that writhes and sparkles
through the destinies hanging on my every hair.

Diana at Lakeside

She stands in tan-warm twilight, still
as the softskinned lake she's watching,
one knee casually bent,

as if those trim sun-seasoned legs
had not been grown to tangle
with a lover's legs, untangle,
then wrap him tightly in.

Her hair carved down to her shoulders
like a brown-gold bell leaves not
a wisp for the wild wrestle
when mouth and hands storm, dishevel.

Who can stare hard enough
to help her feel a cushioned
lover ride the void where now
her lax arms embrace her breasts?

That wound of love that she was born with
sleeps too far beneath the obvious
bikini to be reopened.

Dig fingers and toes in sand, only
drag your glare off her. Her
concealments are easy and still,

as sunset-deep as the long water
she looks out on but not into.

Organon

Let me examine you, she said,
meaning my privacy.
Surprised but glad to oblige
exposure before a woman
I'd never seen before.

And as she pressed and peered
she defined our parts, mine
licensed amateur, hers professional
stretching the pride in bone of blood
another inch of miles.

Thank you, my dear, chaste kiss
on cheek, for something not paid for
by the dollars tucked in her garter.
Knowledge of body, was it, warm
as milk, and lost as in romances, lost.

Now you be sure and come back,
standing like a door in shadow
always ajar. And I've gone back
so many times I wonder if maybe
she's dead by now. Such opening
of the gates, such vigor of practiced buttocks.

My books gaze down at my dog
licking himself. If we could reach
our organs and apertures like that
with our kissing, speaking, eating
mouths, my fellow immortals and I,
would our narrative be worse.

The organ pipes, I seem to remember,
reverberated in heroic chords.
Fat with refuse which those anthems
left behind, the rats of nightmare
roll out from below the pedals.

The keyboard locks, we watch
them waddle to the timbers
of our wistful heaven and gnaw.

Actaeon to Artemis
In the Afterlife of the Art Gallery

"The work of hunters is another thing."

I tell you I never saw you naked.
It was out of fantasy your body carved
for me those supple erotic prayers.
Whatever nakedness there was, was you.

And so in the vengeance of your self-contempt
must my network of reveries harden
and load my head with antlers? Will you
thicken my fingers to caressing hooves?

I see small mercy in your tawny cheekbones,
I see I'll need both hands to pray with.
Consider these hounds of mine, ungainly,
dangle-eared, which I have feathered

like arrows to fly at desperate game,
will you goad them, then, on me
to slash my images of you like meat?
Here at the crossroads it is always night,

even at noonday, and only dreams
can decide. I wait for you to flower
in the full and not the dark moon of yourself.
But fingers already are coalescing,

brain sags heavy with horn. In the distance
which you keep always safe around you
are you leaning and listening toward
your satisfactory wails of hounds?

Undone, Doing

When he helped her carefully undo
her dress, she would not admit
of any but minor creatures scurrying,
would contend how kittens swirled
to hide their eyes in paws of small fur.

When he kissed, lightly of course,
each nakedness unleafing one by one
she still felt only in miniatures
as if to define a shrill of crickets
warming into nooks of an autumn house.

And she allowed gladly,
still in praise of little scamperings,
when he folded the whole body
of love (he called it) completely
over her, fantasy to foot.

She would have argued then
to remember the first-year squirrels,
that they circled grass and bark
and kept balance, twig to branch.
Her mind, bulging with body, fingered

the hard-shelled meats pouched in their jowls.
And some of these (as she lay playing)
she guessed the tiny claws would bury
and forget so that solemn-rooted trunks
might grow to the shade of hickory or of oak.

Evelyn in the April Sun

At twelve years what she wears
allows not half an inch to
ignorance: sweater sharpens the
comedy of beginning breasts to
just a threat of seriousness,
buttocks rounded soft in
brightly flowered pants
parody anticipation so
narrowly they alarm.

When she walks, bell bottoms
ring announcements and no one laughs.

The noon light takes up with her, it
glints electric knowledge all
through her long carefully careless hair while
we stand darkened in our
privilege of years, able
only to know how easy it can
be to make her cry.

A Woman about to Begin

Suddenly, to violate the gently dawning
hills and valleys of your body is everybody's
meaning. Remember, the knight himself
was the visored paramour of his lord's lady,
the confessor a cowled pander who whispered
between seducer and seduced. But how escape,
now the disguises are bold in print
and the real actors everywhere are clamoring?

Who taught you to be ready? Shadows
of complicity are busy behind your gaze.
Drowsing on your eyelash is the animal
you train in secret to devour all ravage
of fantasy and muscle, then wait serene
and still for the delicate pollen touch.

Priapus at the Adding Machine

He has a head to stick in the fire
and from his tail two eggs are jouncing.
From this a dozen daughters may rise
to stand in snow, breathe soot from fog;
or ten sons, to choke on pills and wear
tin collars for prancing through beds of daisies.

Can the women count on fingers dipped
in the bubbling juices of desire? *Do* they
in fact count? Or do their men, for all
their deep voices, count? Billions of asterisks
too far removed in night to betray
their violence are blinking a frantic NO.

Why have the women's milky ovulations
brushed arcs of fury across the zodiacs,
their men slapping at stars like swarms of insects?
Just yesterday the mothers were counting love
by love in the countless leaves which bush
and tree lifted from star-shade into shapes of dawn.

Old-Timer

What a creation he was, made
of old crimes and rags, his mouth
a smear of dirt, a clot of mud
for a heart. Yet words of his
made the boulders shudder for miles
and you could hear wings whistling
from the uncreated springtime
of everybody a child.

Terrified then (you heard them panting)
they tore at their horse's tail of his hair,
they dug at their hell holes in his eyes
until they found his infinitesimal
lightning bug of life and stamped it out.

They buried and buried him (his rags)
and never once could keep him in the ground.
How he seized for instance the basement
furnace for megaphone and whispered along
warm pipes into every room of the house.

He makes no sense, say the elders.
They shake heads in a row along their bench
of watery sunlight, they whittle the soft
blocks of their alphabet to look like testicles.

But the young men must willing sing all night
like dancing in magic circles of girls
whose thighs keep delicate time, keep time,
whose breasts almost hidden in the crackling
bushes of their long hair nod and nod to the sound.

Watchman, What of the Night?

Do you think it has been my pleasure
keeping the night watch year by year,
clutching our common loneliness
to myself alone so you might sleep
in the busy logic of your days?

They are yours too, these difficult lords,
these imps and trolls and the deeper demons
of the long dark hours. And such unlikely
elves and angels as I've encountered
singing their loving mischief have sung

to unnerve the fatted flesh of your
unfaith as well as mine. Would you
believe to feel in our briny blood
the graze of scales where monsters rise
dripping, their alien stares a-leer,

their maws opening in search of us?
You complain of bad dreams but I
defend your dreams against the stench
of hairy beasts buried alive, God knows
how long, among our fathers' graves.

In the bad dream of the news you waken to
do you creep along the abyss of the moment
and hear the hollows in yourself echo
that first fierce stroke of nothingness?
I climb to our bedroom, my ears wild

with chatter of the countless dead against
the booming blood of silence. There
I wait for the dawn of children's voices
running barefoot away from dreams,
for then come tears of sleep to release me.

Love Game

If other ways and kinds of
love fail, try this love-making:
make a poem and get you

lovers you'll never see or
know of, by thousands, hundreds or
three or two. Be sure you

get one lover though,
namely, yourself. Him you
knew only too well

yesterday but now he
shines unknown again and
lights up crowd on crowd that

may be there or not. You
may of course get none again.

Nearing Winter

Two pairs of mallards, tandem,
swim the pond in soundless
march. The males in white collars
search through the dusk of rain,
their motives cold as silence,
their hens brown as November drizzle.

Of such adroit inconsequence,
which is easier to say:
that time stoops down from the affairs
of suns and planets, from the hush
of light-years, to become four feathers

balancing on an eyedrop,
or that this moment listens
to forgive an earth that shakes so
with savage important noise.

Orchestra

O the times now that
God goes out of tune and
praise tames down to
such quaint anthems

even child catechumens ask each
other's eyes, Is this all that
fearsome parent was?

Or the music inflates
altogether out of control.
(At such times watch the
women.) The women

scream their clothes off and
with raped knives hack the
musician into pieces, they

slop his parts still smoking
into the stream. (Listen, in
pieces he welters fluting to the sea.)

Mountains

This quiet of mountains whispering to mountains could demand
    your complete disappearance in the most blatant sunlight.
Winds shake their heads, they'll have nothing to do with these
    trees, not even the tallest.

A road ancient as Abraham's cattle leads your fifty-miles-an-hour
    on and on and says nothing.
Although ear and eye may swivel in every primitive direction,
    they will not detect anything at all
because events happen here like unimaginable sculptures, neutral,
    to one side or the other of every place there is
and they keep no time small enough for clock-towers.

The stillness among mountains has no right whatever.
It may be only the subtlest bones in your own head vibrating.

Suddenly This Left-Handed Life

Look out, we're about to knock something over, knuckles,
knees, elbows, shoulders, hips and feet
stick out in all at once gawky directions,
they bump objects the dusk warps out of place,
we feel them totter, we don't know what they are
except their blunders thud to the bone, familiar.

Our heads however graze tall things altogether
strange, they set them teetering like metronomes
that won't stop, we squeeze our blood small, they won't stop,
they keep on waving at us like hello or good-bye.

Posture

He hammers his tambourine
against his ankles, "not abjectly,"
he says, "but serenely,

risking what my posture
may confess
that I don't know."

His look just shy of pride,
he bangs his rhythms
inside the dance,

he stoops among those bodies
vertical, aswirl, those
upright leapers, snatchers at stars.

The bones of his spirit
he bends down. "The many
mouths of God," he says,

"must breathe along this floor
where feet are twinkling."

May Morning

The young wives trundle their baby-carriages
in the public sunshine of the park, confessing,
childlike, the sins they'd accuse the whores of.

They don't know yet how to wrap their infants
into the prescribed packages of mortality.
They haven't learned how to forgive love.

Hijack

       Picking up
speed
      as if his
trouble
rose to
roar and
scream

he took off
            from the runway
circled once
          the peripheral
reality

      then headed
straight
inside
himself

Views of Our Sphere

We deserved that earth-shot from the
moon's asbestos-gray horizon: a
family portrait on the old homestead, yet
not a single one of us could be
seen and the only history being made was
storm-swirls over rocks and oceans.

So our prophets from as long ago as the
close of paradise had at last a
picture to illustrate their remarks.

As the atoms in our invisible heads
go on blasting out toward darker and
darker lights what can we hope for but
smaller and smaller snapshots of this place
already small and lonesome enough.

The countdown, however, is pulsing in all our
engineered spaces of mind, and each flight
now must explode into the next till
we and our shape in the sun and our weather
vanish altogether (all together).

Up Air

Don't you go out
there and get
lost. Yes ma'am.

Passenger by passenger
safety-buckled to the air
they rocket up.

Where we going, pardon
me, I mean where
we flying?

Don't know but I've
heard stories. So've I. So
why not,

they're telling stories.
You stay in here, hear?
we got places,

we keep hours, by
God you be in bed by
midnight.

How to watch clocks when
Thanksgiving at grandma's
is not a where

at all. Wherever, he says,
we're going, I've heard we won't
go all the way.

You can't go on thinking like
that, he says, try running a
bank like that,

try running a government.
Christmas, shut up, he
said, but I mean

look for July Four on the map,
everybody, he yells, look down
at the grand Canyon.

All right then, ask the
stewardess how far are
we from where?

Well, you might say from the
sun. That's no place to
start from because

I did mean when, we really
did mean where. So you're
trouble-makers,

never satisfied, she says
and camera, her cute ass waggles
down the aisle

like any street anywhere
and when they stretch their
legs, whenever.

Fall Rain

Thunder, old man and
blind, grumbles from
corners. Old too is
rain that keeps falling,

weakly falling, yet
dissolves the roofs over
all you remember into
swamps again, it

will take the sun
centuries to dry them
back into nothing.

Year

Autumn endured beyond rumor.
All around us groves of rainbows
kept promising.

Snow came finally and we were
quarreling with winter
for our lives.

Christmas trees kept falling
down, the sawed roots
slipped at last.

No houses burned, some decorations
broke, a few children knelt to see
how empty these baubles were
inside.

Leaves will return in season
to their lofty perches,
they will inspect us, maybe
judge us.

Memoranda:
from *Agent in the Dark*
to *Central Intelligence*

Monday, Late Evening

Because you have buried dead people
whole for years, no ghosts
interrupt this surrounding dark.

Yet the soil is befouled with souls.
They seethe, angrily invisible,
in the ganglia and at the brain root.

Tuesday Noon

Airline passengers, thermometers
in mouth, rise to such stillnesses
they freeze beyond repair.

Darkened movie houses
and television rooms invite
suicides of ear and eye.

Saturday, Every Hour

One by one, swiftly
invented futures recede
into the present and are lost.

Sunday, 5:42 a.m.

These nights can't be slept in,
the days can't be wakened to.

If Back to Olympus

A lightning bolt of mud
flashes all windows black,
mountains splatter
into space to sound the thunder.

The father's hand that reaches
out toward us goes mad, gives
air to drink, water to breathe.
His lavas hiss and freeze us
into fossils out of time.

Icebergs with our meat
suspended in them tinkle
in his glass like laughter.
He drinks his nectar cold.

Imagine his succulent ambrosia.
Flesh of ours melts back upon
his tongue to when the reptiles
scrambled up from his salted seas.

This is the sacrament
of us he eats and drinks
by day, forgets, and again
by night consumes.

Designs for Sleep

My sleeping marrow rearranges
me again. For what watchers
in the dark do these bone-ends dipped in my blood
trace kaleidescopes of trunk
and branches, swivel-neck and crown?

They shift their contrivances of me
on a bed without edges. Although the shapes
breathe hard, I'm not yet bleeding out.
I stay inside all their changes of design.
Night by night I go in deeper.

Rainy Day: Jogging Indoors

Helps me lift my feet high,
six-shooter tickling my heels.
"Dance, dance, if you want to live."
I do. I dance. Gunpowder
burns up the air I pant for.

Spatters the dust around my feet again. "Faster,
faster, live longer." Bullies the
crowd to laugh, me in my fear
running on old legs in one place.

Tired of the fun, will aim straight
at me, crack-shot and knows where. Will
where matter? because rest for me then
in one place, taste of my blood
cooling in bullet smoke.

Skeptic

I can't believe my hands.
I stare at them open-fingered.
They look like hands I've seen
hanging at the ends of old men,
shrunk into wrinkles, veins distended
like gray blood choking.

When my morning goddess
got me my long youth,
why didn't she also
ask to make me immortal?

Master of Ceremony

Let everyone, he announces, speak a minim
below his understanding and yet be understood.
What else, he asks, are words for?

Divide, he tells us, that space between cloud
and hill by the snow that unfolds down all night.
In what's left over will there be room for the blind
prophet you thought you glimpsed
snowshoeing through an Arctic fury?

Or multiply, he says, the time from thunder
down to valley by speed of rain pelting
the lake-skin to a fur of mist. Will you
that way magnify shorelines to seduce the deaf
singer sloshing barefoot through the rain forest?

Better could we learn, in school or out, he preaches,
how to evade the luxury of sorrow or cure
addictive ecstasies of pain. It's how to shove
the little by little words over the crag
of no statement, no question, as if

you swept the monsoon rain into rivers
or shoveled blizzards into oceans. Isn't it,
ha asks, only below the muscular contention,
below the stretching tight of nerves
where love lives real, down, down?

Lone

When the electric lights went out
and candles refused to burn
and there were no more matches,

he went on drinking wine in the dark.
It was how he conceded his complicity
in the loss of light, with no confessor near him

to witness, interrupt, or forgive.

What to Do at the End

There ought to be something quick
to make a life nearing done
appear.

Maybe a maul to crumble
the slag away in one stroke
and release

a dance in granite. Or,
a veil to whip off so I
can see,

and without my antique face on
my daughter's eyes, can say
to her, look.

Hurry, my son is talking
statements, statements, and I hear
nothing

but questions. Like doves they brush
the window with leafing twigs
pilfered

to foretell his years still deep
in the tide. What to do with
lives

that begin and end shaped
like water. Here I am
my boy,

can you see me my girl.
All I say is quick quick
and like

any drowning child I can
only tell quick means
alive.

Moment

The impotent man answered, 'Sir, I have no man when the water is troubled, to put me into the pool.'

The healing is once only
or not at all, the moment of forever
caged in my kneeling bones.

The people are chanting holy, holy,
around it, the celebrant holds up to it
the disc of bread, saints in the windows
stand painted motionless for it.

Here in my folded palms my stone
melts into me the real name
of who I am and need not ever again
try to be. I have never been away.

My journeys are distances
and times swirling around me.
I will never have to explain.

Belief is me. I have room now
to live in all my doubts.
(There must be joy, that leisure of joy.)

Our gods, human and ghostly, female
and male, have suffered much already
for all of us. Will they rejoice to suffer me
into myself which being past is about to come?

Father Familiar

Gnarled tobacco chewer,
sweated around the yard
and spat copiously into
my mother's bed of
old-fashioned flowers.

So I became in February
and soon after became two eyes
to keep watch on his one
hand could strike in a single
stroke my two ears deaf.

And then grew both soft
nostrils also for nothing but
to record in this world
the sour-sweet of his sweat,
like alcohol, I swore later,

drinking hard for him,
for all that violence in the flowers,
because never took one drink in
all his life the neighbors
shaking their heads behind curtains.

Ten years on and hear me
saying, I'm saying for God's sake
don't die yet, I'm no farther than
those dripping petals in spring,
looking down on his bed,

you can't die yet, you've
got to clean me of the guilt I
still accuse you of, something
has to be said, even written
down, or all that war of

years between us is lost.
But died in his anger
nevertheless. Peace, the nun-
nurse, peace now. But who could
know his fury if I did not

so stooped to kiss and
sure enough the delicate
sweet-sour of his to the last.

Day in June

I was stretched out in my aluminum lawn chair
gazing up at the maple tree that shaded
my car in the driveway, not listening
to our kids playing with the kids
in the next yard, yet hearing them.

I was not dreaming but not quite thinking either
how I'd have to call for an appointment soon
to have my car checked over–carburetor, plugs,
distributor points, and especially that battery
now three, or was it four years old, remembering
like a footnote I hadn't even had the snowtires changed.

Gradually I began to see what I'd been staring at
for several minutes or it seemed it might be for several years:
the whole mass of maple leaves moving in the easy
rising and subsiding wind. When I closed my eyes
I could feel the wind like watching a woman walk alone
in an open field raising and lowering her eyes
and turning her head slightly to this side and that side
as it suits her, who doesn't know she is being watched
and wouldn't care if she did know, through one long
summer afternoon that might be lasting forever.

The leaves, when I opened my eyes, were a different motion, though.
They complicated the wind with contradictions.
Near the top, in the center, there were leaves fluttering
like rapidly shaken bells and they went on vibrating
even when the wind had seemed to die. Lower down,
the leaves suddenly lolled on the solemn nod of a branch
and then as suddenly went back to sleep.
On another branch the leaves were going around, around
in gestures as profoundly mechanical as grieving.

Then without warning, like a dream that explodes noiseless into
    thought,
here they all were, all of them, leaf by leaf, dancing together
    in one dance.
And the one act of sight that took them in required my whole life
and more, and I felt myself sinking, pleasantly drowning from
    hair to toenail
in the tides of salt blood that the muscles of the heart learned
    long ago
from what the revolving moon, long before that, had taught the sea.

There I was in the one act of seeing and breathing, being danced
    by the maple leaves,
driving my car to the office and back, day after day,
the earth twirling the days to each other through moons of the
    seasons,
and I was dancing the dance of love with my wife between moons
and sitting with her at the table after dinner going over the
    monthly bills
until I heard the voices of children in the next yard piping to
    the same dance.

Then it was over. I had not drowned in my own blood, in the
    knowledge of it.
I was sitting in my lawn chair gazing up at the maple tree.
It was then, I suppose, the thinking began but still in a kind
    of dream.
Suppose, I thought, we bring in our most advanced techniques
and concentrate them on this tree in the wind, calculate to a
    hair
the flexibility of stems, the tensions and torsions of boughs,
measure the weights of twigs, the force of the wind, its delicate
    shifts of direction,
its subtle accelerations and subsidences. And then suppose we pour
the organized question of our data into the most sophisticated
    computer
we can fabricate and wait for its answer.

Suppose further that we (turning gradually into they)
call up an imagined head mathematician by long distance code
    number
and ask him to provide an isomorphism from his stock
of models, and suppose, then, they finally arrive at the law
of the leaves' complex motion in the June wind.

I who began as witness, now must rise defendant and hear their
    verdict.
Suppose they judge me the victim of pure delusion,
the dance being not in the tree but on my nerve-ends.

Dragged off to their dungeon of oblivion
I can at least kneel there and give bitter thanks
for my moment of seeing what they having sight
beyond their eyes are blind to, lest they should see. Or suppose
they let me go until their brothers, the analyzed analysts
of the brain, arrive in court a few years later
and decide whether I saw or merely dreamed out
some deeply sleeping wish.

But suppose they say, you were right, our hypothesized data
confirm your surmise. This acquittal is the doom I fear the
    most.
Think of the terrible freedom—to live your whole life through,
hearing the conscience of your vision beating out
loveless numbers for leaves and tides and hearts to dance to.

O my children, sons and daughters of this convicted felon,
you pipe not to the dance which you think is play
but you will have to learn better than he has learned
how to poise your years on the ever finer edge,
having to doubt all things for your minds' sake
yet having to believe for your very breath.

Light as a Quality of Mercy

I

At the end of each short winter day
the dark entered the kitchen
just as the milk came in warm
from the barn. And grandma lighted a lamp

as for some hulking gentle
stranger who had travelled far,
was tired and had little to say.

II

From Elaine's cupped hand a baby
light is born at the candle tip
and you can see its delicate breathing
making friends of the faces around the room

III

The switches flip, one—TWO—three—FOUR,
and light leaps out hard as guns
to occupy precisely the oblong room.

In Pursuit

Gaited to old short fatted
bones of legs, room
to room, upstairs, down,

spins panting, flicks off light
by light behind tall children
(their sunburned marble smiles).

How hands tremble damp
afraid, expense left burning
from space to space where no one

is, five lamps grin
in TV room alone,
pictures talking, no one

left to listen, kitchen
then where no one cooks,
table, no one eating.

Spins, cocktail, damn it,
drools rug to rug, what of it,
through door by door, hurry,

no time left for balance,
children bland by face
flip switches on, blaze trails.

Follows, helpless, hopeless,
darkens, saves, because
not ever life enough

to burn from, how he knows,
how they can't feel it, tall
and smile like statues, as

for instance, this house blazing,
every light left on.

Growing into Light

What can you prophesy, you wonder,
of this child who laughs in her sleep night
after night, hugging her jokes to herself
in the privacy of dream

What cost, you wonder, may the sun exact
for such secret levity when it warms its own
unpredictable dreams into hard being
and she will have to call it a day, Amen.

The Way Down

She was able to kill herself.
She had the strength
and she dared.
But then her hands being dead
could not bury her.
That harder thing to do
she left to us.
It's what we're doing here
this morning.
We may never get it done.

Celebrants

Who'll drink the dead man's whiskey? Don't
all swear at once. Give us time
to count his faithful and their years.

Aunt Karen says besides a quart one
quarter gone he left two more
he'd never touched. Oh hadn't he.

Unscrewed for us the bottle tops
like clowns' hats, his laugh gurgled
in our glasses, we heard it, didn't we.

Drank him for hours and drank again,
maybe by much raising of arms to hurrah
our way to where he lasts forever.

Because he was a miniature, wasn't he?
of the big all-God who got his feet
on the ground at last and when of course

we killed him levitated into rumors
of peace, peace, (and war) repeated
around the earth two thousand years.

So Uncle Emil's blood amber-live
melted all the ice cubes we could
freeze. Yet how somber he glowed

lifted to our mouths for light,
for once not drunk, but being drunk,
and for the first time not good company.

Neighbor: For Twenty Years

I've watched the male strut of her female hips
crossing and recrossing the grass, her arms
yanking hose and sprinkler to always new
dry places. I've felt her blast through summer

like sirens, back door to garage, elbows
bent and arms swinging a stiff six inches
from her body, from shoulders sore with pride.
I confess to her laughter as a habit of my hearing,
she-voiced, crowing raucously over
the neighborhood.

                    This morning tree surgeons
have been felling the willow in the side yard.
Arms folded, she stands presiding over
a log just drawn from the trunk. Quickly
she stoops from round tight buttocks and with flat
of hand spanks the exposed raw white
of wood, slap slap.

Meeting

Don't I know you? Weren't we young once?
Our lithe breaths walked in sentences, I believe,
along miles of country roads, not tiring.
And afterwards we swilled them with beer
like insatiable pigs all night.

Easy, we thought, in sweat of words to talk
our lives-long into shapes that we could love
or at least endure: we were shameless
rubbing our naked wishes against each other.

Now our faces fumble with barely audible
greetings and we turn away. For we have both
been lived by others. At every strategic crossing
those engineers, heads bulging in helmets,
pointed thick fingers at maps saying,
the road will run here. And it did.

Soon, Like Right Now
Poem for a Homecoming

Eftsoons, the poem says,
not even needing to smile,
knowing perfectly well what it's saying,
eftsoons the universe (as you know it)
drops all hands-up and becomes serious.
Already marsupials are invading
paved tundras of the ordinary.

There's an old knowledge, the poem says,
mortared into walls that's thicker
than art. After all, Einstein
elbows out into air, doesn't he?
And hear the salt fisherman
crying, "Kaleidescope, kaleidescope!"
Mountains, believe me, are not lofty

for nothing. Coming home from England
my poet thought he stumbled
on every wave, Greek Neptune
speaking nothing now but the gruffest Anglo-Saxon.

Those Elders of the Great Tradition
&
the Rest of Us

It's as if they dreamed their knowledge
and what they dreamed is what we know.
Who can blame them? They could hardly
have believed this sequel to themselves,
that all their wisdom is really happening.

Yet how can we endure these great grandfathers
of the best we know, who still must sit on every
committee of our thought, who interrupt
our counsels with their wise irrelevancies?
They take their time too, having at their leisure
all history while for us the hour is real.

Dog Drinking at Night

In the darkened house he drinks
and drinks me gradually awake
to a new rhythm happening to water.

Like a fountain at first,
glittering on the ear.
But no—darker, closer to earth,

thirst of tongue that keeps
time to what it thirsts for,
liquid beat, cadence

salted away in the blood.

And dog and man pulsate
to primal wonder like fin and wing
whenever what is needed, is.

The Cricket Sound

Trucks bull down the highway,
double wheels bellow, shake the ground.
Overhead jet-liners howl,
scream low to housetops

yet the September insect din,
thin in the grass as time,
skilled as time, shrills through.

Acres of diminutive telephones
call us from under grass. They ring,
ring, wave on wave, harmonize, clash.

Those crowds, those fathers of ours
have thought of urgent things
they forgot to tell us. Or they've relented.

Or repented. They ring and ring to us
from under grass. Even those first
erect near-men, millions of years
away, have something frantic to say.

They won't get through our hard noisy heads.
Already before snow stills the grass
we are listening as dead to them
as they ring dead to us.

Mail from Home in the Sky

Cozy above us a little airplane chugs
along, all in white. It feels like a pet bird
that knows its home, a throb of our neighborhood
warm in the sky.

                    We watch it turn to slow
pastel pink, surprised yet not surprised.
(Have we, then, begun to remember?) Its toy
motor stills, only our blood thumps the air.

It curves its homespun wings, it's looking
down for a place to fall to and be sick in,
decides with a sudden dip and plunges.
Listening for the crash we grow back down
to children, smaller, smaller, hands pressed hard
but not too hard against ears. When it sounds,
the crash is fur and cotton, we have to hunt
it down past corners limp as water, our legs
are as young as fins.

                  And Mr. D'Arcy's roof
is not caved in, the Hornbacks' garden is not
in ruins. The wreckage lies content among
junked cars in Mr. Garcia's lot next
to the tracks. Fuselage, wings and tail
have crumbled off like sunset, only the tiny
motor grins, intact and dead.

No flame or smoke. The pilot's body has slid
down the smell of hot oil and grease to nothing.
Policemen dressed as important people are poking
looks like x-rays at everything and everybody.
But what can *they* do? Indoors at home we know
that what has happened can't unhappen, ever.

Nearest of Kin

Lucky isn't it that
people
        when they
die
    can't go on
walking around or
talking but

          have to
lie down
        have to be very
still and
    have to be
still
all the time

        because
that way
      we
notice
them

To Frank O'Malley
(1908–1974)

What have you done? You lie so still
you strain belief in our mortality.
We can't believe the body of your ghost,
lithe and fleet, has now been exorcised.

Our scholar gypsy, you haunted the conscience
of all our paths and corridors,
you sharpened with light the shadow that was cast
on what we yearned for in dome and spire.

You christened writers of indiscreetly
visionary words, the baptized
and unbaptized alike, while awed
multitudes of the young looked on.

You gospelled four decades of rich and poor men's
sons showing them where the soul is.
And each day you knotted them thongs to whip
the money-changers from the temple door.

When did you first surmise that yours
must be the gift of loneliness?
When did you discover that he
who is loved by all is loved by no one?

Foreknowing, as you did, such cost of spirit
how did you decide? Or did you?
How can a man, a mere man, decide
to make nothing but himself his own.

There were days we scarcely could endure
for fury of that indifferent love
that smiled or glowered in your eyes.

Forgive us if we found it hard
to quite forgive in you your relentless
understanding of yourself.

But we salute you now as then
with love, across no greater distance
than you always kept, immaculate
and warm, between yourself and us.

Children Lying in the Dazed Heaps of Their Bones

1.
I put the gun of their hunger
to my skull but can't pull
the trigger. My wife's in the kitchen.

2.
In our neighborhood bar a Judge,
a Congressman, or President
foams in every beer.
A General sniffs each glass of wine.
Drink up. Let's go home to dinner.

3.
These old people on television
starving into little bodies
restore us to kindergarten.
We finger our ABC's
waiting like tiger cubs for lunch.

4.
Farmers, listen to your fields
of amber grain tumble into cocktail
lounges in cascades of clinking glasses.

5.
While we were blind with infancy
mother put in our mouths
the cow's tit for her own.
And see how we grew and grew,
sons and daughters of cattle
in the dung-warm barns.

6.
Out here in the open meadow
the tons of beef and lamb
masticated into my tenderly
rounded body begin to low
and bleat against an angry sunset.

7.
Sharp sips of coffee by candlelight
carve the pastry in our mouths
into figures of contemplation.
We chew like monks under rule of silence.

"A Little Folding of the Hands to Sleep"

An old man's sleep is never done.
Every winter night he carefully
stretches his shallow dreams across many wakings.

He hoards all the little yawning times
of days for naps, he saves the pauses
in conversation toward almost imperceptible dozes.

It is never enough.

Those were nights when all night long
the skins of love rubbed fire
from each other like repeated dawns
and sleep was beyond question squandered.

The baby however kept warm for only
two hours in the hospital incubator.
For that brief kick and cry in unshaped
light, din of sounds, sting of touches,
he's been sleeping for fifty-two years.

He still sleeps.

Poem Made Out of Questions

An old woman in a far off country
washing clothes on stones in a little stream
may do the prayer that keeps breath in your body.

And no doubt many old women in wheelchairs
have never been born. But until you can touch fire
and feel only the light, how can you know?

Experts with badges shining on their hearts
are hunting a man whose passion left a girl
dead in the ditch of last night's news.

They train their dogs and lights on his trail,
they search frantically as for hidden treasure,
for the girl's father weeps and curses in his need.

Will he write for her, ever, this epitaph:
love your killer as yourself?

The time for breathing is brief. And you need
years to rehearse hurting before you're ready.
The end of you which you puzzle over and resist,

will that be, then, the reward, a forced
surrender to the imagination of love?

154

Narcissus Flowering

We are riveted and
hinged upon ourself in
such oblique directions

(so many, and not foreseen)

how can you tell
what will happen?

Every day, it could be, you
find an uncle cozy in a
cranny of your blood swishing his

fist of beer almost in
your eye.

Or at table where your
bone crooks into elbow is
sudden room for dozens,

it may be aunts, grandmothers,
who bring coffee rounding to snug aroma.

Consider too how love can
stoop as in those fairy
tales, how we almost say it,

almost on all fours: o lost
brother dog, o sister kitten.

Or at dawn a gauze of
snow smooth over grass, bushes,
tress, exposes such

familiars we are
ready to welcome cousins.

What father, or is it mother,
may focus from an unsuspected
color of our hair or eyes and

claim you then at the ultimate
connection or disconnection.

LATER POEMS
1976–1977

Naked Voice

I overheard you talking in the hangman's office.
I could not mistake your voice so loving-naked.
You must have taken your clothes off as you had done
many times for me, and you were kissing his hands.

You were rubbing his hands hard all over your body
to make sure you absorbed into every pore
their knowledge of sudden, expected, executive death.

The Life and Letters

Whether love succeeds or fails, your love letters
always come back to you, without explanation,
in the same envelopes they were sent in.

Outside the window the faithless moon etches
your maple tree on snow, a silhouette
faithful to trunk, to bough, to every twig.

This tree grew from the summers you grew from
but replicated here in the clarity of winter
if feels as far off as another life, beautiful
as the tree itself, fragile, longer lasting.

Neighborhood Electrification

The empty telephone says
he's gone out to make love to birdhouses.
The entry holes are usually the right size.
If he's lucky enough to catch a bird inside
and can feel the soft feathers of panic
flutter warm against the sensitive end
of his penetration, he expands to such ecstasy
that street lights and house lights for miles around
blaze up to summer noonday
for just the one moment before
they all go out.

Things the Angels Desire to Look Into

What heaven is she the female of,
and I the male, that we act out
our impostures with such heat?

What peace, what balance of soul
are we panting toward and would gladly
give our bare bodies for?

Look out, says the poem,
this may be the last mirage
on death's desert.

No danger. From whiskered face,
from rod and sack I still
cry out in my male voice,

and she is the flesh she wears,
rounded breasts and buttocks,
the delicate cavern her thighs

spread open to, as soft as babies.

Love Song on a Spring Morning

Climbing out from the skin of our bed
how improbable we are!

Who could guess that atoms would imagine
sex as the way to make us possible?

or that chemistry, doubly benign, would make us fertile,
then make us ecstatic victims of our fertility?

Molecules don't say
increase and multiply.

With their sure megaphone of nerve-ends
why take a chance on words?

And hear those grace notes in the leafing trees,
something left over, and for free.

Counting

Stop counting clouds.
Look down, name your ten fingers.
And you'd best look to the women
laughing hilariously together

in the next room. They move
by moon-time as the deep tides do.
If it's sunlight dazes your eye,
you can still count on the women.

For Elie Wiesel

It was different when the triune god
with his shining angels blessed belief.
Now it is only death
that can imagine where our lives are.

All of us are the Jews we kill.
We wait for the holy ones
to speak for us from the fires
of our bones forever burning.

We drink from the bitter pools
where the ashes of our remembering
and our forgetting mingle.
We wait for the burden and the celebration
of our loves.

Where Roar Is Close the Door

When I was barely not asleep,
just there, an inch below nakedness
where I imagined I could still be seen,

the airliner scudded over,
dragging its roar right through me
out of a sudden nowhere.

Through closed lids I saw its yellow eyes
greedy for a landing, its body twitching
red and green jewels of anticipation.

I could plant nothing
in the furrow of smoke left behind
in me before it melted away.

I could grow no thought for those
who sat belted to their seats
as silent as their destinations.

They Are Wicked

They are wicked, I'm sure of that,
but they are gentle. Some of them
sit with me every day in my boat
holding their rods over the side.

They never show me what they pull
up from the deep dark under us
although I ask them many clever
questions. Then they beach my boat
on the dry sand and climb out.

No, no, they murmur, please
don't get up. And they walk away.

The Game and the Word
(For Richard Phelps)

I

It's like making love, finally
you have to be there with your body.
On that rectangle of bed
what good are words?

But you mean the players, don't you,
out on the floor half-naked for action?
Aren't there words in their heads?
And what about you,

aren't you sidelined, a nonbody,
all megaphone, all words from cupped hands?
Listen, it's day after day,
week by week. I have to be there,

I have to muscle my words
onto their bones; their bodies
sweat with the prayers
I lead them in. It's what I'm good at.

II

Look, we lay out a rectangle
somewhere, we floor it with wood.
Earth, I suppose,
is the most convenient,

but it could be on the moon
or on a platform between earth and Mars.
All we need is this oblong of space
hooked into a stopwatch.

Those netted hoops could be catching
butterflies or fish or comets.
The real game is invisible,
like making love. Who knows

what it is? The crowd feels
to me sometimes like all
the people in the world,
cheering, booing, waving

their arms, weaving their bodies.
What private game is each one
watching? All I know is
all of them have to watch

the game I'm good at, it's basic:
five bodies sweating with my words
to get a ball to drop like ripe fruit
into a basket with no bottom.

You could say
imaginary butterflies caught
in nets only half real.

III

These paintings of Van Gogh
at Arles and Auvers: cypresses,
stars and clouds, crows over a field,
twisting, swirling,

muscles of mind tensed
and concentrated in paint.
He was always a point behind
with a minute to go. He had to be there

on that space of canvas
with his body. He had to be there
for the whole crowd of us.

IV

At the party after his reading
you fabricated for that tough old word-artist
(with fifty books behind him)
a swimming pool in the poet's backyard.

We watched him peering
through his thick lenses at the words
you had planted out there in the dark.
We think he believed them.

Alright, alright, I know
what you're going to say.
Let me say it for you:
it's what you're good at.

The Grand Tetons

I

Grown strong with age against those shallow
places where dreams try to control the violent
apparitions of the day, I now walk deeper,

and on my way down hundreds of people
are trekking past me, packs on their shoulders,
in search of the same wilderness.

They are so many they'll have to be very
quiet or the slumber under cities
will wake up and disappear.

Already, quadrupeds, birds, reptiles,
even rocks, cough lightly in their sleep
nosing the infecting consciousness.

II

Why do mountains glare down at us like this
unless the twin minds locked in our skulls
are stolen goods? A free gift of deity,
we once told each other, first having invented
the gods, like ventriloquists, out of our thieving heads.

We've grown wise with feeding on the mind of water, soil
and air and on our plunder of ancient sunlight
in the tombs of fossils. Our fingers twitch with schemes
for tomorrow's pillage. Suicides and murderers fail
to make such news as trees will listen to

because mind cannot repent of being mind.
The gift of robbery frolics in the subways of our nerves.
When, without forgiveness, we outlaw ourselves,
these mountains still stare down at us
through our camouflage of Robin Hood's green legend.

We lie in wait to salvage our own stolen riches
which now rove vulnerable again through the wild.
If once more we seize our treasure, will there be
enough to feed so many, the poor in spirit?

Survival Technique

To survive eating
because your teeth mangle
to death what you eat
or your throat strangles it.

Kill something and eat
because flesh stands on roots
ready to be dead or moves on wing
or foot slowly enough to die.

To drink and stay alive
because clouds and classic
ice wither into water,
vines shrivel into wine.

Because poisons accumulate
in you from multiplied loaves
and fishes, therefore
to excrete, urinate, sweat.

To outlive love-making
because sons and daughters
spring up ready to usurp
your naked ecstasies.

And then to outlast sleeping
because each night
you bleed a little
into what you dream.

Neither Swear by Your Head

Obscure old prophesies push through
to become events that discredit prophets.
Those awesome ones who took shape from nowhere
with miracles of words to doom and bless
drop from our imagining in a rhetoric of autumn.

We see them now as the skeletons
of our own fathers dressed up for Christmas
the year around. Our bones gravitate,
imitating theirs, to resist our lives.

It's not our words clinging to trunk,
branch and twig that weave them into sentences
of trees, volumes of forests. No phrases
we can sound will assemble stars.

However we got here, we are by ourselves.
Let us talk quietly together, then,
while we eat and drink under our frail shelter.

Well, says one, we've got as far
as metaphor and faith. Another asks,
is there more? What all of us know

is that the wind outside is the sound
which silence makes to protest protrusions:
mountains, trees, houses, ships,
and that lifted humming shell, the human head.

Suspended

Times change and that was hard enough
as you could understand even as a boy,
your father still wearing suspenders
in 1941 to hold his decent
opinions up so he could vote for martyred
McKinley every four years of his life.

Yet what is worse is that time changes,
the movie camera crumbles before the movie
of the changing times can be completed.

Your father measured the seasons
on his wrist but left you to contend
with the speed of light that melted
the snow on his fields of winter grain.

You have to answer his voice
speaking to you from the moon
in whose light he planted
everything you inherit.

Believer

Believing in every day of his life
he crossed his heart with the three male gods
of his people, and to make sure, he beaded his ten
fingers along the warm umbilical of their woman.

And yet when he died thirty years ago
I believe he sank into such dissemination
he's too wide now for any recollection, ever.

I say this, says the poem, like a child
fondled on the bony knees of a prophet,
my tongue toying with big words.

The Return

Dig me a hole as big as the earth,
says the boy, where I can keep my things,
soul and all. I've come back to stay.

And so the earth comes back to stay.
The boy's hair by now is white
yet everything comes right.

The boy has proved his mother's
and father's pleasure, he has measured
how a lonely planet loves.

Earth and boy agree on skull and bone,
each calls to the other, Come home,
come home.

The Doppler Effect

One face of the clock is saying,
there's not much time. Finish
what you think you were born to do.

The other rounds and spheres
like sleep, it questions
over and over, what is time.

Did we pass through winter
or did winter pass through us?
You creak your windows open

to this familiar green clutter
called the spring. But nothing happens.
You only change places with yourself.

And Your Old Men Shall Dream
with Their Hands

I

I have sung my hands before,
how they have taken hold
of steering wheels, doorhandles,
handles of lawnmowers, hoes, beer mugs,
have picked up pens, papers, books,
and have caressed dogs' backs, cat fur,
the long hardbreathing nose of the horse,
women's silk-skinned bodies,
and my own flesh blunt with bone.

But now I sing more loud (I think)
my same two hands held open
out in front of me, palms face
to face, two feet (about) apart.

And I confess I'm all fingers
tingling with this feel of nothing,
amazed at what my nerves
can touch, my only hands
squeezing this specimen of space
between them, this ghost
fertile with galaxies.

II

Is this the best use of hands,
or only the last? The poem
may be fool or prophet, the words
tightly tentacled onto the blank page
of our hearing. Yet you or I
could pick them off like locusts
and hungry as we are for silence
eat them into nothing.

But for now we listen to the empty air
between our faces echoing our one mind.
It may be the only mind there is.

A LATER DAY, ANOTHER YEAR

1977–1988

Entrances Haunted by Exits

Dialogue at the Door

I had no intention
of coming this way again,
but here I am. Do you
still have light for me?

Yes, but not as bright as before.

And the darkness?

Not as deep and dense.
Expect sleep to be
foreshortened, dreams more shallow.

Has this place become
more narrow, then, than it was?

No; in fact, much wider,
but air is thinner.
Muscles of mind and body
have to breathe harder.

Well, then, shall I come back in,
as if beginning once more?

Dear old friend, it's not
your choice. You must.

New Acquaintance

At the bottom of the stairs
I glimpse my body, for the first time,
as an outmoded model of me.

Surprised, the most I can promise is
that up there in my bedroom I'll undress
him, fit him into baggy pajamas,

roll him into my bed and fold him
into my sleep where we can dream
memories together or not dream at all.

Prayer for a Seemly Stance

It means help me now not to stoop
with the retrograde inclination of joints
and bones and consenting muscles
toward the postures of old men which my limber
youth could enact precisely on the college
theater stage but could not foretell.

Seventy-Fourth Birthday

What is new? I've been mortal all
my life. It's only that now I suspect
where I have lived is where I live.
Ancestors are many layers deep,
too deep, too many for me to count.

A voice in the cool of evening searches
through a faulted garden. It nags
at the eroding gravestones: "What
was your crime?" "We were for many years
alive but at last got caught."

At the Kitchen Sink

After the last dinner dish
is rinsed and dried,
the faucet, turned off,
continues to drip.
It should not be allowed
to tick away the seconds
of something as precious
as a lifetime. Yet is does,
it does, it does.

How Time Is Kept

In the flurry of our beating hearts
there is never time enough for what we dream of.
Our intimate dead, however, lie calm of face
as if to say, no need for hurry.
They idle in such a wealth of stillness
it can never be wholly spent.

Yet they are close, deep in our one affair.
Don't disturb us, they say, we are busy
at the leisure of not breathing. It takes all
our time, it takes more time than being alive.

Old Man Looking Ahead

Maybe it's only one final fact,
much smaller than you expected,
which then will slip into place, to complete,
not the answer, but the question.

And you with your coronet of darkness
to make you invisible, your wallet
stuffed with the relics of your own bones,
given that responsible grace

of keeping fresh the uncreated
stillness, not even needing
to know that without you
the silence would be imperfect.

Journey through the Cloud of Unknowing

This morning in his seventy-ninth year our friend
proved his mortality and so became earthly whole,
leaving us behind, not yet complete, able

only to imagine his flight on an instant wavelength,
neither up nor down, and no longer outbound but inbound,
back to the first impulse, and there to undergo,

together with all his galaxies, an implosive
annihilation, and in the first blink of extinction
to discover that during the eons made of swirling,

exploded fragments, his true place, from the start,
reposed intact in the unbroken body of nothingness.
How could he have dared to foresee it? to be drawn

unerringly into a total idleness as innocent
of every wisp of created being as it was before
the beginning, nothing but glory now, and he

completely himself, transfigures into praise,
all his words outgrown, his grammar obsolete.

What His Nurse Heard

Minutes before his death
he said
I'm glad
I had good teeth

To Get the Most out of a Hanging

This stairway leading you up was not
constructed for your coming down.
The few makeshift steps you climb

were meant to dwarf whatever height
you may at times have dreamed of. When you're
manacled, hooded, and the false floor

caves in, it's arranged that your own weight
will jerk the rope strangle-taut, giving
your love of life the abrupt look of a suicide.

Neo-Scholasticism, 1980s

How many viral demons
can dance on the point
of a needle, or the tip
of a penis?

A Journey of the Mental Traveler

Resurrection from a body where I had spent
my life proved harder and took longer than expected.
The scalpel-spear all but bled me away
into my sac of urine swollen, drop by drop,
as from a leaking ocean. Diminished to an impulse,
I had to swim, holding my breath, through sea-salt
miles of arteries and veins until a limp heart
surrendered me to lungs slowly forgetting how to breathe.

But here was air, it lifted me tall enough
for brain to open ears and eyes, rouse naked
intimacies of touch. Tongue was loosened
to answer the sound of my pseudonym by which
I could recognize myself though as yet unnamed.

Yet parts of me have been left behind
in obscure nooks of cells and organs.
People and things have grown so compactly real,
so intensely present, they caricature the wide
echoing estates of time and space I afforded them
when I was living, I thought, the true story of myself.

I search such sleep as I am given
for a dream of quiet talk with Mary
and Martha in their garden. They, endowed
with wombs, should know better than he, how well
their brother managed a second life, a second death.

For Men Only

The lab report: "Well differentiated
Adenocarcinoma, Gleason Grade iii/x."
Both doctors (M.D.) agree that nothing
needs to be done, that there's nothing
to worry about, that these atypical
cells, though mad, typically sleep
where they are, like Rip Van Winkle,
for twenty years or so.

Still, "Adenocarcinoma" does not
translate well in the dictionary:
"A malignant tumor originating
in glandular tissue"–for example,
the prostate, for example, yours.

The doctors find especially
good news in "Well differentiated"
and in "Gleason Grade iii/x."
And what can you do but nod
your head in profound sympathy?
They belong to *you*, after all,
both the crazy cells and the sane ones.
Who are you to differentiate?

The Prowler

Why bolt the doors and lock the windows
of your immunity when he has tools
of entry shaped like parts of your own body?

You remember a few anxious times when you
caught glimpses of him (or her? or neither?)
skulking around shaded edges of your inheritance.

With your first open look at his face,
what if you recognize the earliest friend
of your birth, aeons older than mother and father?

Then it would be out of wonder at his diligent
devotion to you that he takes your breath away.

In Bed Alone

For just a moment or two
I've been allowed to be
only what I am now,

relieved of all thought
of how or why I got here
or where I'm going. And believe

me, this thing that I am
is small, small. A problem
hardly worth sleeping on.

My Two Lives

The life I could have lived,
that other, better one,
is also mine. Who else
can claim it? Each morning, stooping
down, I know that I'm not worthy
to tie my own shoelaces.

The Son of Man

Yes, when taken down, he'd been nailed,
hands and feet, his side pierced, but his
legs were not broken, and how many miles

he has trudged, back and forth around
the earth to torment and redeem
the last twenty centuries of our existence.

A High-Toned Old
Christian Gentleman

One detail from the shadowy scene
tells us his posture: his naked toes
are pointing straight up, the soles of his feet
press against nothing more solid than air.
He has for the moment lost his foothold
on the earth where all that happens is real.

And yet he does not go climbing up
the air to heights where grave events
would release his body's weight to all
he could imagine. He is simply
sleeping. His toes twitch with dreams
not in the world but of the world.

Genesis 7:27

"And all the days of Methuselah were nine
hundred sixty and nine years: and
he died."

(This is surely going to great lengths
to show that old age does endanger
your health.)

The Night after Sleep

After the party he idles toward
an hour of reading in his bed
to invite sleep. Prompted by habit

he flicks off lights in kitchen,
dining room, front room, thinking,
"I won't be back this way till morning."

And what an immensely accurate fact
lies secret as a seed in this casual thought
until the miniature dark that sheathes his sleep,

bursts into the one all-containing night
which millions of stars have labored
for millions of years to illuminate.

GAMES NOT TO BE TOYED WITH

Behind Home Plate

This television super-slow-motion
replay shows us the pitcher's fast-ball
floating so lazily toward the batter
we can see the seams revolving.

We can hardly believe the sweat
the pitcher is wiping from his brow,
or the batter's miscalculation in striking
out. It gives us a glimpse of what

it is we measure in clocks and calendars,
how it bulges with both absolute speed
and absolute stillness beyond our knowing.

At Center Court

Backcourt to backcourt
the ball whips flat
across the net by an inch
or ovals over in a top-spin.

Now the players converge
at the net, their racquets
turn animal, the ball leaps off
instincts bared to the quick.

For three hours we've watched
them sweat their bodies to invade,
to defend, one arm lengthened
to sting or caress the air.

At last they are being applauded
into sweaters along the sidelines.
What remains is the stubborn
geometry etched on the same ground

we all walk on. It is still divided
by a wall we can see through
and stretched tighter than nerves,
strung on muscle-frames, can bear

for more than a few hours in the sun.
These rectangles laid down rigid and white
as bones along the packed earth are not now,
are not even a game, are always

a later day, another year, younger bodies.

By Firefly to Tokyo and Back

In July twilight a galaxy
of fireflies twinkles low
across the darkening lawn.

We watch in awe. For them
a labor as inescapable
as the orbiting of stars; for us

silent fireworks celebrating
our patch of earth. They look
like the chirpings of birds we heard

in the half-dark of early dawn.
The distance from birds to fireflies, from ear
to eye, is made from the stuff of lightyears,

but the jetliner winging us to Tokyo
and lighting us back again
only gains or loses sleep.

As always, a matter of dreams.
The belly dancer writhes to her music,
the children go on chanting their games.

Translating the Latin

We were inching our way through *De Senectute,*
a page or half-page at a time. One by one,
in a sequence of our names we never learned to predict,
he called on us to English the Latin we first
had to read aloud. Scanning our scrawls sequestered
in the margins of our page and cribbed from the best
translations we could find, we spoke in the meek
deferential tones befitting our plebeian rank.
("The noblest Roman of them all," our yearbook called
     him.)

Did we ever fool him? We knew that he had heard
our plagiarisms hundreds of times before.
But never once did we guess how deep a game
we all were playing as he listened alike to the worst
and best dissemblers among us. What he heard
must have been that persistent music of old age,
not his, not Cicero's, but ours: a sonata
of the years which only our banal young voices
could compose and which he alone could hear.

How much he could teach us now, trapped inside
our grammar of shrinking sinews! Those suble inflections,
for instance, to fortify our subjunctive or conditional
moods against unwarranted indicative statements;
those periphrastics to guide us safely around
the things we should have learned and forgot;
and those inversions of time which we now surmise,
subjects deferred years after the events of verbs
have commandeered their objects, direct and indirect.

But in surviving we have come to feel almost
at ease with the imperfect syntax of our lives.
We no longer have the will to rememorize
the niceties of our conjugations and declensions.
Besides, he is still ahead of us, some fifty
years beyond old age. What he might teach
us now and in what language we cannot imagine.
All he has left with us is our next assignment,
not telling us when it is due or what it requires.

Evidence

I can't talk to you now,
says the bank robber. Later,
says the killer, I'm in a hurry.
The landlady says, My, my, it's true
they were always going and coming
at all hours but paid their rent on time.

What stays still on the courthouse clock
is the same as what moves round and round
its face. Camera tapes for the evening TV news
revolve, revolve, trying to find a center.
The landlady, it turns out, doesn't know where it is.
The Judge by mistake smashes his watch with his gavel.

Metaporn

Our pornographers have discovered, not
meaning to, that nudity now befits
our tribe as it did at its chilly beginning,
a complete exposure of ourselves before
it's too late to confess; before, that is,
we all have our clothes blown off.

But what an excessive disrobing we've invented,
down to the marrowbones, the soft moist genital
pleasures seared away, leaving exciting positions
of insertion and reception only to be guessed at
from bare skeletal structures. Supposing,

of course, there'll be any leering eyes left
to ogle those pelvic precincts where sons
and daughters found partners, century
after century, to re-enact the naked
bedded antics of their fathers and mothers.

Solitaire Lotto

Suppose, for instance, a someone who
has wagered prayers against so many
years that words and numbers have worn down

to gestures like those of the infant he once
was, blind fragile hands challenging
the empty air. Then, when wakened

by sirens speeding into and out
of earshot, let him cross himself
or merely raise a hand in the dark:

a random quest for at least one other
in dire need somewhere in the world
for whose sake whole cities may be spared.

Natural Relations

Gardening through the Ages

A sudden whiff of the spoiled fish
which you forgot to bury
in your garden warns you of
the body you are, or own.

Yesterday when sickling
last year's weeds around
the lilacs, you sliced through the tiny
bones of a bird, still feathered.

Before that, you spaded up
black soil poised between
leaf-shapes and anonymous humus.
It smelled of old secrets unearthed.

II

Eat my body, he said,
given for yours. Then fingered
the loaf into twenty centuries
of crumbs as fine as dust.

Pity the harsh poverty of belief.
The rich young man turns away
in sorrow, the rough fisherman weeps
when the body, come from the tomb

to the seashore, waits to share
with him the broiled fish to ask
three times, Do you love me?
Then feed them, fisherman, fish them.

And what assurance for Magdalen,
forgiven, but weeping inside
our garden? Do not
touch me, the time is not yet.

Smell of Survival, Long Range

Blood and brain can do nothing with this primitive
scent skimmed off ground soggy with November rain
except to whiff you back to some child of yourself,
maybe to that first slap that tingled you into breathing.

Or farther back? Say, to baby fish, or bird, or reptile
jostled into the pungent savor of an old earth's morning?
Old men learn to forget so much, it may be
they can detect the odor of memory itself.

So wait. Under these dripping leaves of the oak
that grandfather planted, stand still and wait.
Over there from the brambles stirring
at the garden's edge may appear

some weasel-shape with enough cunning
of smell to stay visible among the living.
If nothing be seen, a squeal or squeak may open
your ear to what has long been in the air.

Birds, Chimneys

When we knelt at the cold fireplace to listen
closely, we heard no hint of song, no cheep, no chirp,
only an intermittent flurry of wingtips
against the masonry trying for flying room.
The hoarse whisper of feathers scraped
at a sooty underside of bird-life unknown to us.

A prolonged silence. But when we opened the cast-iron
damper, instead of a dead or half-dead
defeated lump plopping into the ashes
of last night's grate, a live projectile
shot out, as if a rocket launch from our tall
chimney had gone berserk, had backfired
into a crazy zigzag of curves, swerves,
dips and upswings through front room, dining
room, kitchen, study, sunroom, sometimes barely
missing our heads, bouncing off the false promises
of light in windowpanes, but never once resting,
untiring wings determined to translate
our walled-up spaces into outdoor meanings.

At last it found the door we'd been holding
open for it until the whole house was freezing,
and all we had left to do was to look for droppings.
What we found was a trace of soot on one white curtain.

Twenty-two years later on another day
that falls five degrees into the zero of winter
we look out our windowpanes to see
cardinals, doves, juncos, sparrows,
and even a few tough, scornful jays
warming themselves on the rims of our neighbors'
chimneys. As they huddle there, fidgeting,
adjusting their feathers, they warm us too,
just as they are, just as we are.

Winter Holiday in Sunshine City

This indolent wind fondling
the fronds of palm trees chafes
the conscience of my northern skin.
I detect a warming in the wanton
pleasure that tingles up
to me from bay waters mouthing
and tonguing the naked beaches.

In a sudden fantasy as savage
as hunger, I am lugging my body
through white drifts, my own warm meat,
heavily wrapped, steaming
from nostrils in a frigid wind.

Is there a touch of grace
the blood needs in having to learn,
one season each year, that time
is driving toward absolute zero?
If so, what a pity, after
so many winters, to miss
even one such fragile favor.

Mid-Winter Greetings

Dismiss the wide gray face
of sky; it expresses nothing,
is almost absent.

Stray flakes of white
meander down, so few
you could count them.

Starlings in a dark cloud
drift into black branches
of a distant treetop and become
so still they can't be seen.

Dead leaves left hanging
in the nearby oak quiver
in a breeze as brief,
as inconclusive as a sigh,
then are dead again.

The snow of last week's
blizzard lies flat
on its back. Its rigor
tightens the arctic cold.

There's barely movement
enough to keep time
alive, the faint tempo
of waiting for nothing
that can be spoken.

A postcard picture of winter
Lotus-land. It tells you
that peace is infinitely
desirable, that only
the dead can endure it.

Mountain

To have a mountain you need a lot of room.
Also a solid base because a mountain is heavy.
And you should have some sky to spare
because a mountain hoists itself up
into a permanent snowy season taller
than July, disturbing your horizon.

Though you might spend your life here,
to presume you could domesticate a mountain
would be like pretending you kept a dinosaur
penned up in your backyard as a pet.

However, from a proper distance you can
sometimes gaze and gaze at a mountain
until you feel yourself leaning upon
its craggy, primitive hide as if at home
in its long resistance to earthly weather.

And a mountain makes it hard to be
afraid the world might disappear
while you are being still and merely looking.

Interrogation

You watched the alleged
disappearance of the sun
which people call sunset?

Yes.

Where were you at the time?

I can only say I was
where I continued to be.

What do you mean?

I mean I know I was not
where that tall pine was,
a short distance away, because
I saw it vanish into total darkness.

How did it happen?

Like the rest of the landscape
it faded without a sound.

But you felt the wind brushing past you?

Yes.

Do you think the wind
was implicated in the loss of light?

It wasn't strong enough.
It touched me gently, cool
and refreshing after the hot day.

You've mentioned that faint
but incessant barking
of a dog in the distance.

Yes.

Did it sound to you
like a warning? Or perhaps
a prophecy fulfilled?

I think the dog was barking
for private canine reasons.

You've said the birds fell silent.
Were they concealing things
we ought to know? Would you
suspect them of complicity?

No. They tuck their heads
under their wings only
to secure their own bird-dreams.

Where were the birds hiding?

I don't believe they were hiding.
They were nestling in the trees for sleep.

Did you see them there?

No.

Then how do you know?

I don't.

Quandary

When you push the emptied dishwasher
back from the sink to its resting place,
its wheels don't squeal as usual. And through
the open window comes a cool
breeze, a parting, patronizing
caress from the torrid afternoon.
Yet your day does not close whole. You recall

how quarks of all colors, all nuclear spins
and forces combine to query, as if
they are quibbles, the very questions you strain
to raise at your utmost stretch of mind.
Should you, then, look for unexamined
quirks in your bundles of nerves, or for
unexpected wobbles in the light from stars?

The Twister that Missed Us

A flash of thunder has stunned our electric
clock on the kitchen wall. At dawn
it circles astray in a vanished night.
Once losing the scent of our fugitive hours
this pointer we trained finds only us.

Do lightning-propelled wind and rain
have a father? There must be a family
language which they obey, gibberish
to us, but for them as clear as touch.

Huddled in basements candle-lighted
like catacombs, what was left
for us to pray to except the ring
of stillness riding at peace in the storm's eye?

Incident in a Rain of Violence

For a man about to be struck
by lightning the broad sky
is no different from a dark alley
where a pistol takes aim at him.

Experts in the law will find
this fatality "an act of God"
with no blame attached.

Astronomy

It would seem that loaded
with the debris of suffering
accumulated from the centuries

of our history the earth
might become too heavy
to spin accurately around

its axis. The quite recent ovens
of death-camp crematoriums,
embracing the flames of Hiroshima,

ought to be enough to clog
the earth's smooth parabola
around the all-seeing sun.

And yet according to our own
meticulous scrutiny our planet
continues to perform like clockwork.

It must be that in the breathless
lofty spaces through which
it moves, its burden of human

misery becomes weightless.

FAMILY RELATIONS

Tricycle

Behind the frisking, farting tail
of our young mare, Nellie, we were riding
the seven-mile stretch of dirt road
from the "burg" back home to our village.

Wedged between my knees was the tricycle,
hatched at last, shiny-real, from the page
which I had kept warm all winter long
in the Sears and Roebuck catalogue.

My father was slapping the reins against
Nellie's rump, and when the hurried
wheels bounced in and out of the caked-mud
ruts, he would yell, Watch out! There it goes
over the side! And I would grab
the handlebars and hang on hard.
My mother said, Will, stop teasing
the child like that. But what did she know.

The enormous sunlight of that whole summer
held still and firm, I thought, all around me
while I pedaled my three wheels up
and down our brick sidewalks so fast I saw
the spokes spin into one flashing blur.

Even so, I could fly no faster than the Twentieth
Century Limited which I was driving
at full-throttle, whistling my mile-a-minute
disdain at boy-size towns like ours.

Yet I was straining toward that orgasmic
peak in time where speed explodes
in a tower of fire, and beginnings and ends
of rails and sidewalks melt into one moment.

My own children were clinging to my back
like laboratory monkeys. They stared
ahead in terror at speed as pure
as instant sunlight, knowing they could not
let go of their primitive father-flesh.

Incident in a Long Story

Gathering from her clothesline the billowing
bundles of her half-dry Monday wash
into her arms, my mother shouted to me
to rescue my tricycle on the wooden walk.

I got astraddle of the metal frame
just in time to scream with the thrill
that exploded through it, a close echo
of the lightning bolt that scarred
forever the trunk of our neighbor's great elm.

In that split-second I learned I wanted
to live, one flash bright enough for a lifetime.
As if God had said with destructive emphasis:
I tell you what I told myself at the start,
that all that I have made is good.

Watching the Nightly TV News

I feel for my belly button.
It is still intact, firmly knotted.
There's no escape; I've been born,
no matter how many decades ago
my father and my mother died.

Recent Family History

Looking out at us from their photographs,
mothers and fathers, aunts and uncles,
now dead for forty-five years or more,
don't recognize us, can't even imagine us.

And we are helpless to penetrate the safety
of their innocence, leaving us to become
the alien, diminished species, Treblinka
having taught us that to be alive can be

a capital crime and Hiroshima showing us
how most efficiently to execute the criminals.

Love Song in a Minor Key

It's not this harmony of naked
bodies clasped together, the moist
blood-swelled thrust fitted
into blood-swelled orifice.

What perfects their night of love
is something they know they both fit into,
like the ancient dark that drifts in
over them from the open window.

It's something they were born with
but can't possess. As if each one
had mortally wounded the other
near the beginning of time,

and now they've found in this duet
of such bodies as are left to them
a way to claim the sweetness
of their hurt if not its healing.

Eileen and the Daylilies

I wonder how my glance, hardened
by years of falling on rows of brick
and stone buildings, on metallic lines
of traffic, when falling casually
on her, melts into air which I must
breathe into me every moment to stay alive,

and how the air darkening in my veins
must be driven through my heart and breath
to be restored so that I can see her
in our garden, all new, as she fingers
those gracefully curved blades of sunlight,
the lilies that will live for one whole day.

Her Wealth of Shells

Back home again in her heartland she's picked out her best.
She arranges them on a sidetable like a showcase of jewels.

She remembers the night she wakened to the bay water
shaking the air, its whole body a froth of whitecaps,
its bare fangs tearing at the sand and the seawall.

The next morning it wallowed in a bath
of sunshine. Its mammoth weight,
lolling about, lifted a gentle overflow
of ripples along the shore. And then

as if this salt-water monster had casually
tossed it to her, there at her feet
in the wet sand lay the prize
she's been looking for for weeks–
a King's Crown, perfect in every detail.

How could such a clumsy, amorphous
giant teach its little soft ones
to spin from their gelatin bodies these exquisite
private castles, hard as stone?

Now they are here, spread out before her:
ribbed, whorled, voluted, turreted,
in patterns artfully imprecise,
striated or speckled with bands and dabs
of color, smooth as polished gems,
or pebbled with whims of warts and pockmarks.

Granted, the elemental need to survive,
but why this excess, what need to be beautiful?
She tries to imagine how much her forebears
had to forget, aeons ago, while learning
to make her human. One by one

she fingers the shells with names she has had
to learn, like a child, from picture books:
cockle, pecten, whelk, coquina, tellin.
Those with punning nicknames sound
closest to her: tulip, cat's paw,
cat's eye, auger, worm shell, olive.

She watches the landlocked light wither
to mere husks the fabled treasure
she meant to bring home in her plastic bag,

yet says amen to the space that has been given
her in air, on dry land, where she has room
to love them if not to know them. She picks up
her King's Crown. The sultry midwestern
afternoon sweats salt in her hand.

For Eileen on Her Birthday: Walking with Her around Saint Joseph's Lake

She drives the car but when we park,
she hands me the keys to carry.
Before I can knock out my pipe
she has crossed the paved road
and stands ready like a traffic cop
to signal me a safe moment to join her.
Then she bounds down the concrete steps
as if she's going to hunt something
we can bring home to eat for dinner.

We stand together on the path that will
revolve us around Saint Joseph's lake.
She announces our starting time.
Although her watch is faster than mine,
I say nothing. For a few paces
we exchange banalities about weather
and temperature, and then she is off,
soon ten yards ahead. After we have rounded
the boathouse curve of the path and are
coming to the weeping willows
I run to catch up to her and make
some hard-breathing comments
about the patterns of shallow waves
woven in the water and the nuances
of cloud-colors reflected on the dome
and spire on the other side.

She has already observed them
and maybe dismissed them.
She begins to talk about details
of foliage and flowers along the path
that I haven't seen. I lag behind.

By the time we get to what is left
of the woods I wonder if the joggers
who pass and meet us know we are walking
together. They greet us separately.
Maybe they think I am chasing her.

I am. At the tall colonnade
of walnut trees she is out of sight,
until I see her sitting on the steps,
waiting. "Although, looking back,
I couldn't see you," she says, "you're only
three minutes late." Space and time.

I think back to my many years
of illusion: me sitting still
through long hours but striding
through thoughts and images
of muscular language builders
of books while she lay sleeping.
The race between tortoise and hare,
but when Saint Joseph of the Lake
tells the fable, which is which?

Last night, calling from Los Angeles,
our daughter asked me, "Did you ever
think you'd be married to a sixty-eight-
year-old woman?" But our daughter
was inside our marriage for only nine months.
I try to think from the outside, like her question.
But it's beside any point I can make.
Instead, I try to think, What if
her mother had never been born? I can't.

In the innocent parabola of the path
around Joseph's lake there must be hidden
some mechanism that betrays little
but means everything. Like a clumsy
geared wheel meshed with intricate
accuracy into a smaller, faster one,
for no reason, except that it works.

I try to imagine myself circling
the lake alone at my own pace,
greeting the joggers with a nod,
but never geared to anyone at all.
I can see only incalculable disasters,
like suddenly, in mid-stride, forgetting
how to walk, or plodding around
and around in a void with no one
sitting on the concrete steps
to tell me when and where to stop.

Daughter Departing, Arriving

She's nearing the narrow canvas tunnel that opens
into her flight. Her hand and our hands
winging farewells from above our heads, have already
signaled the rift between airborne and earthbound.

She disappears inside, leaving us only
this whimsical shadow of herself, a giant
facsimile of a bird sprawled on the tarmac.

We must wait, it seems, for minute
after minute to mount a montage of glimpses
at all her twenty-nine years before this stiff-winged
monster consents to lumber sullenly into place
on the takeoff runway, diesels faintly hissing.

Here too we're compelled to linger, to be taught again
how tedious suspense can be, as if our nerves,
though aging, could forget the growing gravity
of the nine months that weaned her out of hiding.

And now, abruptly interrupting all time past,
blind turbines, trained by touch with the runway,
are assaulting our common air, demanding flight.

(Isn't this fabricated promise to lift
her human weight above the clouds too *loud?*)

But with only a few heartbeats of pavement
left, the air complies with an upsurge
in our lungs like a newly invented way of breathing.

And this gawky, contrived creature rises
into as lovely a bird or angel as poet
or mystic ever conceived. Then dwindles
to erase the vanishing point of our scene.

Why have we stayed on for this still, invisible
moment, if not to listen again for her first
birth-cry and from there to follow her
through our everyday habit of breath and pulse
to the very brink of the heavens and (who knows?) beyond.

We turn from an empty sky
to face each other. A quick laugh
confesses we've both been caught
indulging in the substance of things half-seen.

Our mutual guilt links us helplessly
together. Arm in arm we leave for the parking
lot, then home. But what is home until,
two hours later, the telephone rings?

She is down to earth again, tired and hungry.
We barely have time to ask, How was your flight?
Bumpy, she says, from Dayton on, but the landing was perfect.

What Can "Grand" Mean?

Here is grandfather with his granddaughter
on his lap. They are reading aloud, sometimes
in unison, more often taking turns,
from a child's alphabet book, big and small
letters repeated in pictures and words.

Back to his ABC's grandfather
is old enough to know he is where
he belongs, just now beginning to learn
the rudimentary but difficult lesson
that he was born to die. He's surprised

how easily from the same gaunt letters
he can teach a child warm in his arms
that she was born only to live.

Should the daughter-mother suddenly
come upon them now, in the folds
of the overstuffed chair, she might wonder
if she had caught them in a pre-creation
scandal, nestled together in one womb.

FELLOW TRAVELERS

Time and Again

Young men and women
visit us, their eyes, their faces
fresh with life as it is now.

They bring us the glad news
that we've been allowed
to live for a while with them
in their unknown future.

Resistance

When your eyes begin to blur
the lively distinctions of color
and shape in the things around you,

as if complaining, Haven't we seen
enough? And your ears, weary
and bored, neglect the finer

modulations of meaningful
sound in speech and song;
and your feet move reluctantly,

even for short distances, heavy
with many trivial and futile
destinations, you must

not acquiesce. You must
resist, not to retrieve
yourself but to rescue the young

who wish with the same passion
you once were filled with, to live
as long as you have and longer.

Oldest Guest at the Celebration

These youngsters in their thirties, forties and fifties
are no longer amateurs of life, but the luck
of living still shines in their eyes with such
easy intensity it warms you to be
crowded among them. As they talk with you

you hear their words blend into songs
you recognize as from a distance.
Do they echo old neighborhoods
where you have lived, or the unknown place
before you? Of both? It may mean only
that you are becoming slightly deaf.

What does it matter? You are here.
Drink your wine and listen. Enjoy the party.

Injunction to the Young

Don't abandon your elders
(already weak with age)
to their burden of inherited

ignorance. Jaded as they are
with the luminous discoveries
of their youth now fading into

clichés, they are as vulnerable
to new knowledge as kindergarten
children and are as easily

enlightened or deceived.

Gerontocrats

We wear our years like a badge
that envelopes us from head
to foot, recognized everywhere–

thinning white hair, wrinkled
face, sagging shoulders, slow
cautious gait. What it

conceals is that our selective
order is by nature
compelled to induct all
who live too long to protest.

CAN THESE BONES LIVE?

The Story Lost in Words

One midwinter morning he finds
that he has lost his ancestral Bible.
Hours later in the dusk of twilight
he's sure he has uncovered it
from under his pile of disheveled newspapers.

But his study-lamp reveals his error:
the book under his thumb is a dictionary.

It's as if the whole law and the prophets,
Pentateuch and Gospels, have crumbled
into bits and pieces, mere words arranged
in a mad, meaningless alphabetical order.

Surreal and Real

Although you were barely prompt enough,
you did glimpse time blending into space
in Einstein's brain. But luckily you
didn't throw your watch away;
because it's Newton who has remained your closest friend
and neighbor.

First Day, or What You Will

He thinks there must have been an unplanned
micro-delay in the big explosion which launched
existence into space. That explains, he says

why everything since then is slightly time-
flawed, happening a little too late (or sometimes
too soon which is too late turned inside out).

A Still Noise

There once occurred a silence,
all dark and odorless, that commanded me
to halt and listen. How could I refuse?
And now after so many years ago

how can I remember what I heard?
I have waited too long: the dead
have become too many and too explicit,
and the living suspect nothing.

When I got out of bed this morning

When I got out of bed this morning
to join our human tribe, it felt as if
we were all moving together through
our calendar-defined parade of days.

Until I felt someone stepping on
my heels. I thought it must be
a stranger. But looking back
I understood how he didn't even

see me. How could he? He was
myself of sixty years ago
when I was living forever every day.

I must have become a ghost haunting

I must have become a ghost haunting
the several lives I've outlived, a disguise
to protect me for a time from that identity
which is as fatal as history.

A Blip on the Magnified
Computer Picture

On your way to the barbershop
you're almost blown off your feet
when it occurs to you that you're
using some of the very same time
needed to keep the galaxies
spinning through the light-years.

In this once country graveyard

In this once country graveyard,
now caught in the tentacles
of a noisily expanding city,
we can feel more intimately than ever
the heavy demands made upon us
by the dead. Here they stand
idling, day and night in the din
of traffic, as mute as time
itself, as still as stone.

They require nothing less
of us than our lives.

Don't spend too much grief

Don't spend too much grief
on burial grounds and their inhabitants.
Save some for yourself. It's a good investment.
Already you begin to see satisfying results
for everything that lives,
for everything that dies.

College Yearbook, 1931

How can we forget how eager
these professors were to disturb
our young, unexamined lives
with their own ardent doubts and beliefs?

And now here they lie as if
snugly tucked into their graves.
Did they find no further place
to go than here into our mortal memories?

Close your wings, bright angel!

Close your wings, bright angel!
They expose me to light which I have
not as yet learned either to absorb
or avoid. It only threatens me,
do you understand? And it hurts.

September Afternoon

Crisp wings of butterflies are creating out of
nothing but air, caverns of fish
pregnant with the mind of eagles.

Can we imagine that some strolling dream
of ours as dull as sleep itself stubbed its toe
on a nub of nothing at all and exploded
us into where we are now, looking around
and wondering?

Jack and the Beanstalk

I've tried to pry myself upward
with extravagant prayers
but as I near my last days (and nights)
I discover I've reached only the rooftop of the house
I've lived in all my life

And to tell the truth
I really can't see much more from here
than I saw from some of the more
modest elevations below.

"Can These Bones Live?"

Ezekiel 37:3

From the clock I've always lived in the presence of
but have never seen I sense a warning
more intimate than touch that I am nearing
the event which is as desperate as birth.

Small wonder, then, that I have misgivings.
For instance, I've never been taught how to crawl
out of a human skeleton decorously and with skill.

If only I could remember how I managed
to infiltrate this nest of bones
in the first place—
but I can't.

Old Man Lighting His Pipe

Once a year you smoke your pipe
in season; we call it Indian summer.

Tobacco, the Indians' gift to the white man
to rot his lungs and forked tongue,
a delayed revenge for the paleface
gift of rot-gut firewater and firearms.

You imagine those Chiefs of the Indian Nations
seated in a solemn ring, passing the pipe,
one to the other, their news of peace rising
enlarged, in smoke signals, from hill to hill.

Now you see smokestacks and the exhaust
pipes from miles of traffic sending up
diffused, unreadable signals, city to city.

Children, no longer amused by the smoke
rings you can blow, are blowing bubbles,
galaxies of spheres, shining, floating
with no need of fire, on air as still as peace,
then exploding noiselessly on the green lawn.

Memorial Day

On this day every year
our dead afflict us with
a kind of solemn astonishment
at how close to us they remain.

The dates on their headstones
reveal that even in their graves
they grow older year by year
just as we do. They are still with us.
We are all going in the same direction.

Christmas, Year after Year

On this day which we proclaim God
has made we forgive the poor for being
always with us. We pardon them
with baskets of groceries, bundles of used
blankets, outgrown coats and boots.

We recreate them in our own
image for this one day, making
them warm, well shod and well fed like us.

Impasse

His fourth-grade teacher shouted
at him (in class) "Answer me!"
He knew she meant to say, "Anchor
me!" because she had been
floundering in deep water for some
time, maybe all her life. His
hair stood up on end because
he was only a small boy not strong
enough or smart enough to rescue her.

When I woke up this morning

When I woke up this morning, I counted my fingers
to test those bewildering, repetitious dreams
of the night. There were still five digits on each hand
including the two opposing thumbs needed
for grasping things, sometimes so intimately
that things feel as naked as nothing but thoughts.

I wonder, could the tail I abandoned millions
of years ago have gotten itself reconstructed
into that invisible, prehensile thing
I swing around inside my head?

A Summer Solstice Long before Now

It cost you only the expense
of a single puckish summer night
to discover that elves, pixies,
or even old-fashioned angels
can't lead your life for you.

They are too inexperienced.

The most they can do is exclaim
in amazement at your follies,
then gasp in wonder at how
you manage to escape, your life intact.

Trickle Up?

Does human evolution have a future?
Even our dog is troubled by the limited
significance of our presence. He whines
at the door wanting to get out.

His Local Habitation
without a Name

When we found him drinking our furniture polish
he explained quite simply he had run out of beer.
It was not so much the taste which exhilarated
him, he admitted, as it was the ruddy harvest
color. And finally there were those words printed
on the label like a rubric, "An end to dust."
And wasn't it dust he would soon need
to be delivered from?

A Brief Story of Time,
Outside and In

When he comes face to face with the kitchen clock,
he crosses himself because he's old enough to know that early
or late it's time that threatens him.

And now he can sit and listen to the night outside.

What he hears first is the unceasing, merciless din of traffic
along the nearby highway punctuated
with dissenting sirens. And then from across the river

he detects the church tower keeping the faith,
storing each hour away, melodious quarter by quarter.
What is left for him to do is listen for silences

within himself deep enough to resonate into one
inexpressible meaning the fury of the pavement
with the meditative bell.

July 4, 1991

Please don't inflict your flag
on my defenseless body. I have
an old horse blanket that
keeps my blood warm on the
coldest nights. The horse himself
galloped away some years ago.

An Arbor Day Anniversary

The tulip tree lifts its flowers up
like a host of candles to be
lighted by the infinite blue sky,

and we can feel our earthly afternoon
come alive with blessings
in every tingling pore and cell.

At night it is her dreams

At night it is her dreams
that drive her silently
across the vast fantastic
regions of her sleep.

and when she wakes
she finds that they've
returned her to her bed,
her pillow scarcely ruffled.

She wonders if there could be
a morning when her dreams
might lose their way and fail
to bring her back again.

At what outlandish place
might she be then forever stranded.

Mother's Day Greeting

My longtime lover and wife, receive
this gentle May-morning rain as if
it were my gift to you on the day which
our public calendar decrees is yours.

Only you and I know that my feigned gift
of rain means our grateful loss of the
many long dry seasons which we had
to endure before these beautiful new

people consented to appear and
complete our lives with theirs.

After Fifty-Seven Years Together

We can only wonder how lightly
we have left behind, one by one,
the different love affairs we have had
with one another.

           During this pause
before all memories fade, by merely
touching hands we can celebrate
our loyal infidelities to those
passing lovers we once were,

now most precious to us but then,
each pair in turn, threatening to become
as fixed as the end of time.

An Affair

It's the light of a full moon that invades
her sleep but her dream persuades her
it must be bird or bat, her bed
being so near roof and rafters.

It's a soft terror that holds her,
downy and feathery, a prolonged
near ecstasy like a frustrated
orgasm. It leaves her pounding
a velvet door which conceals
nothing but the silence of light-years.

When she wakens, all she remembers
is secretly holding hands
with the foamy pale water
of the fountain in the city square.

The Scandal of the Rainbows

At the foot of this morning's rainbow
we found no pot of gold, only
a pat of butter waiting
for our late breakfast.

Of course, after such a long
history as ours of eons
spent in darkness, we
have learned to expect

our days to emerge more
modestly into light than those
father Adam named into being
and Uncle Noah, ages later,
had to rescue from a mountain top.

Early Resources

I still remember when my body
and I were playmates, perfect
equals, head to toe. While still
crawling we shared secrets which we

kept strictly to ourselves as
the gentle unsuspecting giants
went on crooning over us.

At the Beach

When she saw the naked imprint
of his big toe in the wet sand,
she wondered if it was an indicator
of his physical endowment.

All the next day it filled her
with the most pleasing surmises.

Gave her a toe-hold, you might say.

A Stranger, Coming and Going

She has a face
too sweetly innocent
to give fair warning
of a derriere
so provocative.

Episode: July, 1920

One summer afternoon when he was
twelve and his parents had left him
alone in the house, he stripped off
all his clothes, crept out the back door
and raced down the brick sidewalk
to the family privy at the lower end of the yard.

And waiting there in the half-light
were those grown women in the slick pages
of the Sears and Roebuck catalogue,
dressed only in tightly fitting underwear.
They kept on smiling straight at him
even when he showed them how
completely naked he was, all over.
Why did it please him to know
that they could never be friends of his mother?

But what did they really want of him?
He lingered with them as long as he dared
enjoying more and more the danger
he was in of being caught without his clothes.
After his panicky flight back to the house
he was trembling and breathing hard.
It was then he got scared. For the very
reason that he had nothing he could tell them
he wished mother and father would get home soon.

Rites of Passage

The girl bass-drummer in the high school band
banged out the punctuation of the Sousa march
with such fierce emphasis he felt exposed
as if she had shattered the playpen
where his mother had put him fifteen years before.

And when she crashed those cymbals together
he was ready to fall at her feet and plead for mercy.

How could she do it, her face so sweetly gentle,
her slender figure so lightly graceful?
He had to know, he had to see her alone,
perhaps in a private booth at Pearl's
Ice Cream Parlor. But how could he ever ask her?

What if she might accept?

How History Is Made

"My God!" cried the Princess, "take your hand
off my knee!" And she was right, of course.
Because it was history they were in, after all,

and if his twiddling fingers had been
permitted to go on exploring the enticements
of her more intimate clefts and protrusions
who knows what might have happened
to all the arrangements the future
had already made for later memorable
battlefields and famous speeches printed
for schoolbooks growing children might
memorize and recite for generation after generation.

The Gloomy Corner

is formed out of a deep basic
weariness below the level of sunlight,
yet "dark" is too innocent a word
to name it. The slight tinge of guilty
involvement hinted at in "gloomy" is needed.

This structure of elusive intangibles
is best built during an afternoon just
bright enough for the gloom to show through.

A room inside a room is as old
as your childhood when you threw
a blanket over the backs of two chairs
opposite each other and then crawled
into the cave you had made. You felt
oddly at home, strangely secure.
You were already too old to remember the womb.

The gloomy room has a couch but no bed.
It's a place of rest you've spent your life
creating. It's not a marble slab in a morgue
nor the tousled sheets of wild pleasure;
only a gentle place of disciplined dozing.

Must I ask of every terror

Must I ask of every terror
that assaults my sleep:
are you from hell or from heaven
in disguise? What is it

comes out of the dark
to wound my private sorrow?
Is nothing sacred?

Waiting for a Twitch of Prophesy

It's only a light-switch away.
But it's still dark, very dark,
my friends. I have to sleep
in order to remember your names.
Strategies like heart-beat
and breathing are involved.
I hope you understand.

Aristotle in December

I feel special pangs of pity and fear
for those called upon to die in winter.
It seems a reckless, brutal addition
to the fate of all the rest of us
deeply doomed enough already.

Higher Mathematics

The benefit of living beyond eighty
is that bone marrow and every nerve end
begin to tell you that all your decades
however many will add up at the end
to total loss.

Any Questions?

While trying for over eighty years
to become real have I been learning
nothing but nomenclature? that wife,
children, friends are only nominal?

Be careful, old man, such impolitic
queries come close to the quick, can
draw blood. Just below the skin
lives an animal whose deft pretense

to honor your grammar may turn
to treasonous, dangerous deviations.
What you hear along the sidelines
are hounds howling, tomcats screaming,

donkeys braying. Are *these* the answers
to the questions your years
have kept on asking and asking?

Now after eighty years of life

Now after eighty years of life
I discover that all
I have wanted to do
was to write a poem that would love me,
all the way through my pretenses
but without pampering me
like the spoiled child I suspect I am.

Yet how hard it is to accept gifts,
especially when they prove to be necessities,

like friends and lovers
and enemies and death also
even though too stupid
to do or say or feel
or think anything at all.

Last Chance

Each spring for eighty-two years
you have survived the brutal
green and flowering onslaught
of new life in everything around you,
from the humble grass to the tallest treetops.

And still you stumble around in the same
stupor of ignorance you were born with.

You're approaching what may be
your last chance. If the violence
of death, attacking you in every
cell of your body, can't wake you up,
what in Heaven's name can?

If, after eighty-four years, you run out

If, after eighty-four years, you run out
of faith, don't give up hope
which may prove to be the only
real resource you've ever had.

In fact, it may be hope as naked
of tint or color as the air itself
which alone can smuggle
you into your remaining years,

and, who knows, may even ease you
with all the innocence of love into that vacancy
beyond time which we have never learned
to measure, not its beginning and not its end.

Soon after Nightfall

Watch the old codger toddle off
to bed and to his lullaby prayers
which he has no more need to understand
now than when he first heard
his mother murmuring them.
It's the wisdom of the Elders
descending from generation to generation.

The Spell

Watching night come on after
a whole day of steady snowfall
is a story of someone dying
all your life long among white sheets.

You could nudge yourself
to make sure it's not you
but you know there's no need.

A fool of the late autumn night

A fool of the late autumn night
he stumbles indoors, slamming the screen
behind him, his hair full of cold
rain, his head full of clouds
whose end and meaning
he knows he will not have time to decipher.

Let me assume some far-off

Let me assume some far-off,
long-ago space in time where
I met inadvertently a creature-song
as inescapable and persistent
as destiny. It was music I am
only now beginning to hear
although I must have been humming it
to myself all my eighty-five years.

Birthday

Imagine the hubbub
among all the people,
some not yet even imagined,
when he announces,
"I'm going to be born
tomorrow!"

A few cry out, "Already?"
Others warn, "You'll be too early!"
"Or most likely too late,"
mutter the elders, losing
interest, already dozing.

Since I've lost some of the hungers I once

Since I've lost some of the hungers I once
needed to survive, beautiful fish come
cavorting into my easy sleep merely
to amuse and entertain me along the way.

Now I Lay Me

On my way to bed
I whisper to the clock
on the mantel (or wink)
Because I'm hoping the air
between us, being deaf
and blind will soon let me
dwindle softly into the warm
timeless nowhere of sleep
(without, of course, letting
me blunder into spaces
too far and deep to waken from).

How humble our history is!

How humble our history is!
a long line of ancestors unknowingly
growing these heads we wear
from the bloody paths traced
by their tails.

Final Exam

Was this what we were meant to grow into
through those millions of years—
creatures that can name all things
around them and so build a second
creation out of nothing but sounds
in their throats and mouths? Has Adam

then (our old namer), actually identified
nothing, being only a doll
on an unknown ventriloquist's knee?

Quiz Show

Small children can ask you
without words, simply by staring
at everything around them including
you: All right, we're here. What
happened? Where do we go?

Thirty years later they're
saying with an excess of words
and gestures (sometimes violent):
All right. We're still here. What's
next? The best answer you can

give from what you've learned
in three decades is this: it's
childhood all over again but with
a difference: the meanings get simpler,
the words get harder to find.

Twilight

A pair of spectacles and a pair
of hearing aids are at rest
on the dining room table like dice
in the posture of a loss we can't interpret.

We know that all the clues we once thought
we had are aging into a second ignorance,
though not as innocent as the first.

What we long for now is a simple
miracle. Not a heroic deed of the mind
but a brute bodily fact as for instance:
"One thing I know: I was blind and now I see."

At last we have learned that time
is always relentlessly modern.
The heaven that the angels sang
had melted back into common stars.

Was the hound of rescue, then,
that pursued us down the years
only the sound of our own hard breathing?

Our long parade of years is drenched
in silent farewells performed under dripping
graveside umbrellas. Mud it was,
but still we said, dust to dust, with one hand.

Is that sound you hear only
an inquisitive wind in the eaves
or the mutter of prayer wheels and beads?

Gentle lies are being told under the hill
almost in whispers. No harm is meant.
Twilight is beginning or ending
something as accidental as a seed
dropped from the beak of a bird
returning to its nest at nightfall.

There's an emptiness widening
in the weather and a mild wind
pressing us as close to nothing
as we can get without dissolving.

But only at the absolute, soundless
end may we hope to learn that
there is no end, that whatever
else he may be, God is no atheist.

315

"Do Not Go Gentle"
A Posthumous Note to Son and Daughter

If, at the end, I seemed
to depart too willingly,
don't be distressed: I was tired,

not of living or your love,
but of being incurably old.

Acknowledgments

The author makes grateful acknowledgment to the editors of the following publications in which these poems first appeared:

COLLECTED POEMS: 1953–1977

American Prefaces: "Hospital" (© 1938), "Armistice with Doom" (© 1942).

Choice: "Whan That Aprille, Etcetera" (© 1961), "Day In, Day Out" (© 1961), "Watchman, What of the Night" (© 1962).

The Commonweal: "Peter and John Running" (© 1955), "Crisis on the Hill" (© 1955).

Contemporary Poetry: "Sweet Killer" (© 1954).

Heartland II: Poets of the Midwest: "Mail from Home in the Sky" (© 1975).

The Hudson Review: "Vacation Land" (© 1958), "Faith on Friday" (© 1958).

Indiana Writers: "Children Lying in the Dazed Heaps of Their Bones" (© 1976), "The Way Down" (© 1976), "Old-Timer" (© 1976), "Priapus at the Adding Machine" (© 1976).

The Iowa Review: "Celebrants" (© 1971), "Fall Rain (© 1973), "Light as a Quality of Mercy" (© 1973), "Mountains" (© 1973), "The Poem as a Private Persecutor" (© 1974), "The Poem Dresses Up Like Love" (© 1974), "The Poem Is Showing" (© 1974), "The Poem Out on a Night Mission" (© 1974).

The Massachusetts Review: "A Plaint of Flowers" (© 1960).

The Minnesota Review: "Evelyn in the April Sun" (© 1969), "Rainy Day: Jogging Indoors" (© 1969).

The New Yorker: "Parked Car" (© 1938), "Child" (© 1957), "Nearing Winter" (© 1966).

The Ontario Review: "Designs for Sleep" (© 1974), "Dog Drinking at Night" (© 1974).

Poetry: "Etherized Intelligentsia" (© 1943), "Lore of the Real" (© 1943), "Survey on the State of the Union" (© 1943), "The Chase" (© 1946), "The Unhappy Warrior" (© 1946), "Communion" (© 1948), "New Age" (© 1948), "At the Mercy Seat" (© 1949), "Anecdote of the Wind" (© 1949), "The Hurt of the Second Death" (© 1952), "Standard Time, Ithaca" (© 1952), "The Word and the Fish" (© 1953), "The Improvement of Prayer" (© 1955), "Toy Windmill" (© 1955), "On the Adoption of Sons: An Anniversary" (© 1955), "Pater Noster in Winter" (© 1956), "L'Après-Midi d'un Homme (© 1956), "Last Things, I, II" (© 1959), "News Item: Chimpanzee Escapes from Zoo in Antwerp" (© 1959), "Bus to Marien-lund" (© 1959), "Surgery Ward, December 8" (© 1959), "Day in June" (© 1965), "Growing into Light" (© 1968), "Those Elders of the Great Tradi-tion & the Rest of Us" (© 1968), "Her Poem" (© 1975), "The Poem as Baby-Sitter" (© 1975), "Survival against the Poem" (© 1975).

Poetry Northwest: "What to Do at the End" (© 1969), "In Pursuit" (© 1975).

Prairie Schooner: "Portraits" (© 1958), "The Change of Seasons" (© 1958).

Prism International: "Love Game" (© 1970), "Organon" (© 1970).

Saturday Review: "Views of our Sphere" (© 1969), "Hijack" (© 1970), "Sud-denly This Left-Handed Life" (© 1970), "'A Little Folding of the Hands in Sleep'" (© 1971), "The Cricket Sound" (© 1971). *Notre Dame Scholas-tic:* "Diana at Lakeside" (© 1972), "Narcissus Flowering" (© 1972), "Or-chestra" (© 1972), "Posture" (© 1974), "Undone, Doing" (© 1974).

The Sewanee Review: "Logos" (© 1957), "Childhood Scene Revisiting" (© 1957).

Shenandoah: "Nearest of Kin" (© 1970).

The Yale Review: "Subway Train" (© 1954), "Moment in Suburban Summer" (© 1954).

A LATER DAY, ANOTHER YEAR: POEMS, 1977–1988

Cedar Rock: "By Firefly to Tokyo and Back," Fall 1984.

Konglomerati Press: "Winter Holiday in Sunshine City," December 4, 1982.

Michigan Quarterly Review: "At Center Court," Fall 1982.

The New Republic: "Smell of Survival, Long Range," July 4 & 11, 1981; "Tri-cycle," September 6, 1982.

PN Review: "Gardening through the Ages," 1981; "Old Man Looking Ahead" 1981; "For Eileen on Her Birthday: Walking with Her around Saint Joseph's Lake," 1984.

Poetry: "How Time Is Kept," August 1978; "Interrogation," January 1984; "Seventy-Fourth Birthday," January 1984; "Translating the Latin," January 1984; "A Journey of the Mental Traveler," December 1986; "Dialogue at the Door," December 1986; "The Prowler," December 1986; "My Two Lives," December 1986.

Poetry Northwest: "Birds, Chimneys," Autumn 1982.

The Wallace Stevens Journal: "Quandary," Spring 1985; "A High-Toned Old Christian Gentleman," Spring 1985.

CAN THESE BONES LIVE?

Poetry: "A Late Twentieth-Century Prayer" and "Soon after Nightfall"
Arts Indiana: "After Fifty-Seven Years Together"
America: "Old Man Lighting His Pipe"